What people are saying about

Otherworld

A fascinating blend of science and spirituality, of past and present, *Otherworld* is animism through a contemporary lens. It embraces various folklore, from different perspectives, and creates a way to interpret the connection between these older beliefs and modern magical traditions. A wide ranging and thorough discussion of both the theories ar   iw-to, this book will undoubtedly be useful to many '   ι 21st century perspective.

Morgan Daimler, author   *'ic Fair Folk* and *A New Dictionar*

In *Otherworld: Ecstatic \   ɔpirits of the Land*, Chris Allaun offers a comprehe   u illuminating overview of the magical universe, drawing upon Celtic and Norse myth, folklore and experience, as well as drawing upon the insights of other cultures, discussing faeries and elves, animal spirits, nature spirits and techniques of shapeshifting. The book focuses upon two main themes close to my own heart: the connection of the magician to the land, and the expression of ecstasy as a magical technique. Most importantly, the book is clearly and fluently written and is first and foremost a practical work for hands-on practitioners.

Michael Kelly, author of *Aegishjalmur: The Book of Dragon Runes*

Chris Allaun presents a wonderful book that taps directly into a subject that is very close to my heart and my own magical practices. This is all about working directly with source magic from the land. He covers some interesting angles and shares his obvious experience and practical knowledge. A fascinating read.

Rachel Patterson, author of several books on Witchcraft including *Witchcraft into the Wilds* and the *Kitchen Witchcraft* series.

There are many books about the invisible or intravisible side of earth (aka the "otherworld") as mythical, metaphorical, and magical. But, few are written by a human journeyer who has painstakingly trained and shifted their awareness using the lore passed on through literary and oral traditions on how to enter, encounter and exchange with the otherworld and its "secret commonwealth" for the love of earth and her life. Christopher Allaun is one of the few. He has demonstrated his otherworld competence and experiences in the living HHevelopment to set the tone, which in my view is sacred magic devoted to the wellbeing of our world and its life. From there Allaun gives a menu of magical treats offering techniques including dance, breath work, shape shifting, traveling/ flying and more. Then he provides the benefit of seeing through many cultural lenses that it is populated with an array of powerful intelligences such as Jhin, Faery, dragons and more, and he shows them as the powerful, wise and crucially important "original ancestors" that they are. Why is this book important to the health of humanity, and even more importantly avoiding the oncoming ecological disaster and a human-induced mass extinction event? To do this, we must go to our roots, our foundation, our planet - for we are children of one mother and her name is Earth. I grew up with an old Appalachian saying "you cannot bless the fruits and curse the roots". This wonderful book leads us through the visible structures of earth into its "pre-formed energetic, plasmatic and starborn original state" to recapture our place in the emergent destiny of our garden of Eden. In doing so,we awaken the memory of the original instructions pulsing in all of Earth as "the life that runs through all" and the old magic returns with original innocence, co-existence and co-creation and restorative life. Read this book. Internalize its wisdom. Become ignited with the ecstasy of life and wield magic with muscle for the sake of all. All for the Love of Earth.

Orion Foxwood, is a self-proclaimed "Eco-Magical Activist" and, a Traditional Witch, Southern Conjure Man, Faerie Seer and Founding Elder of Foxwood Temple. He is the author of *The Tree of Enchantments, The Candle & The Crossroads* & *The Flame in the Cauldron* with Red Wheel Weiser Publications and *The Faery Teachings* published by RJ Stuart books. He founded the House of Brigh Faery Seership Insitute and its 7-year Apprenticeship program.

Allaun's book presents an engaging and eclectic mix of traditional practices, supported by useful exercises for developing sensitivity and skill.

Diana L. Paxson, author of *Trance-Portation and Possession, Depossession, and Divine Relationships*

Otherworld

Ecstatic Witchcraft for the Spirits of the Land

Otherworld

Ecstatic Witchcraft for the Spirits of the Land

Chris Allaun

BOOKS

Winchester, UK
Washington, USA

JOHN HUNT PUBLISHING

First published by O-Books, 2020
O-Books is an imprint of John Hunt Publishing Ltd., 3 East St., Alresford,
Hampshire SO24 9EE, UK
office@jhpbooks.com
www.johnhuntpublishing.com
www.o-books.com

For distributor details and how to order please visit the 'Ordering' section on our website.

ISBN: 978 1 78904 534 5
978 1 78904 535 2 (ebook)
Library of Congress Control Number: 2019955406

A CIP catalogue record for this book is available from the British Library.

Design: Stuart Davies

UK: Printed and bound by CPI Group (UK) Ltd, Croydon, CR0 4YY
US: Printed and bound by Thomson-Shore, 7300 West Joy Road, Dexter, MI 48130

We operate a distinctive and ethical publishing philosophy in
all areas of our business, from our global network of authors to
production and worldwide distribution.

Contents

Other Books by Chris Allaun

Underworld: Shamanism, Myth, and Magick
ISBN: 978-1906958763

Deeper Into the Underworld: Death, Ancestors, and Magical
Rites
ISBN:978-1906958824

Upperworld: Shamanism and Magick of the Celestial Realm
ISBN: 978-1906958923

Introduction

As you walk through the deep green wood you feel a slight chill in the air. Twilight has come to the forest and as the day's light dims, the shadows of the trees become darker. You can see the colorful display of the sky as the sun sets. You know you must get home. Soon, the forest will become too dark to see and nocturnal creatures will come out to play. The sound of cicadas fills the air but you know they are heralding the coming darkness. The sun is setting more now and this is the balance between day and night. The in between time. Walking briskly through the forest, you feel a presence. If almost feels like you are being watched. As if someone else is there watching you walk away. You turn around, but you see no one. Strange. You could have sworn, for a brief instant, that someone was watching you, even following you through the forest. But you see no one. You continue walking and the forest seems to come alive. Perhaps it is the glowing gold of the setting sun, but the trees, plants, and the stones seem to be coming alive. Finally, you make your way out of the wood. Somewhat relieved, you turn to look back to the darkening forest and part of you yearns to be back there with the beauty of the green wood. And the wood, in turn, yearns for you....

The Otherworld is a place of magick, mystery, and enchantment. It is the place that is beyond our physical world and is home to many beings such as Elves, Faeries, and Nature Spirits. It is so close to our world, but for many, it is so far away. In the type of Traditional Witchcraft, I was taught, we worked very closely with the Otherworld and the spirits that dwell within this magical place. I was initiated into Traditional Witchcraft by my first magical teacher, Matthew Ellenwood. He taught us many powerful trance techniques and introduced our circle to the powers and beings of the land. As with any good teacher, Matthew has the skill to bring his students to the magick but allows them to discover the magick all on their own. It was because of the many full and dark moon gatherings that I began my practice with the Otherworld. Many of the theories and practices I will give you are shamanic in nature but are seen through the worldview of the Traditional Witch.

There are many different types of Traditional Witchcraft. Some are more ritualistic than others while some rely purely on connecting with the energies of the land and performing magick based on intuition and the guidance of the spirits. In this book, I will go over the lore of the Otherworld and the many spirits you will encounter. The purpose of the book is to teach you how to deepen your relationship with the powers of the land and the Otherworld; to truly walk between the worlds in order to heal yourself, others, and the land itself.

We begin the book learning about the creation and evolution of our Mother Earth and life upon her. We must start our exploration where we are; the natural world. To have a deeper relationship with the land, we should first begin to understand how she was formed and how life evolved from the depths of the sea. Through learning about nature, will we learn of her healing energies. We will then learn about the lore and magick of the Otherworld. This is the place of great mystery and the realm which contains the great life force that creates our physical world. We will learn to navigate the fantastic world through the lore and stories told by the Celts and Nordic peoples. In order to make contact with the Otherworld spirits, we must learn trance techniques that use the natural rhythms of the land. By the exploring ecstatic dance techniques of Native Americans, Bushman, Whirling Dervishes, and the Traditional Witch's dance, we can learn to tune into the pulse of the land, to go into trance and gain entrance to the Otherworld. There is also a dance that conjures sorcery and allows us to reach into the Otherworld to perform magick and divination: Shaking and Swaying Seidr. This is a powerful technique that allows us to go directly to the

Otherworld and perform our magical rites.

Once we gain access to the Otherworld, we can begin meeting the beings who call this wondrous place home. Nature Spirits help us heal and are a part of the magical web of life. We will learn to deepen our relationship with the spirits of nature so they may teach us to heal the world around us. Spirit Animals are powerful beings who can help us connect to the animal world. Witches have connected with the spirits of animals for hundreds of years. Through establishing a relationship with animal spirits, as well as our own personal Spirit Animal, we will learn to tap into great healing power. There is a secret power that witches have with animal magick; shapeshifting. Throughout myth and lore, the witch has the ability to change shape into any animal of their choosing to work magick, heal the sick, and commune with the Faerykin.

We will continue our path deep within the Otherworld and meet the Elves and Faeries. Many times, the Elves and Faeries are elusive to humans. We have lost the trust they once had for us many years ago. In this section we will learn to create relationships with Elves and Faeries and rebuild the trust that was lost. Through this we will learn of powerful healing magick from the Shining Ones. Our final destination with this body of work is the Dragon. They are powerful beings who direct the regenerative life force of the land. They are creatures who have the power to create or destroy. We will learn to establish relationships with dragons so that we may learn of their wisdom, power, and healing energies for ourselves and the earth.

In this book I use the term *Spirit Walker* when referring to shamanic practices instead of the general term Shaman. I have found Spirit Walker better conveys the type of spiritual work and magick that we are performing in our everyday spiritual practice. There is some lively debate in the pagan community about if it is correct to use the word "shaman". Many feel that the term is appropriating a title that is specific to the Tungus or Evenki people of the Siberian region while others feel the term has come to mean a type of ecstatic spiritual work that is performed by the healer. I can see both sides of the argument. Personally, I like the term Spirit Walker because it conveys precisely what we are doing as healers and earth-based magical practitioners; we are walking with spirits. Unlike some magical traditions, we are not commanding spirits or even asking them for services. We are establishing deeper connections with them so that we can have a synergistic relationship. I have come to understand that the best way to work with the spirits of the Otherworld is by working to open our hearts and energies to them. By doing so, they will teach you many magical skills that humans can never teach you. By establishing a regular practice with these spirits, we can return the balance between our world and the Otherworld.

Chapter 1

Mother Earth

"The Earth is your Grandmother and Mother, and She is sacred. Every step that is taken upon her should be a prayer." Buffalo Calf Woman, as said by Black Elk in *The Sacred Pipe: Black Elk's Account of the Seven Rites of the Oglala Sioux*

Nature

When we look at nature we are looking into the heart of spirit. The rising sun uses its magick to dispel the darkness of night. The warm winds that comfort us come to us from spirit. The depths of the oceans are enchanting yet the waves come crashing to the shore with a warning of her power. The forests are alive with animals and birds who sing of the earth's sacred beauty. All things are born of nature. All things live their lives in nature and when they die, they return to nature herself. The earth is a mystery and she is sacred. The Earth is our Mother and she is holy. Take a moment and remember the beauty of a sunset. What feelings and energies do you remember? Take another moment and bring yourself back to a time when you were in the forest and were surrounded by beauty and life. Or a moment when you were on top of a mountain and were in awe of the grandness of the earth itself. We have all had moments when nature made us forget about our day to day lives and sent energy to our hearts.

Through evolution, all life comes from the oceans and the earth. We are born of the womb of Mother Earth and when we die, we shall return to her womb once again. She is the mother who brings us life and yet she is the mother who cradles us and welcomes us into death. The earth is healing. She provides us with healing medicines and shelter from the day to day weather. It is from her body we take trees, stones, and other materials to build our homes and shelter. It is from her that our food is grown so that we may be nourished so we can live. She provides all things and she is sacred.

All things that are natural are magical. Every rock and stone. Every tree and plant and every animal that walks upon the earth, flies in the skies, or swims in the oceans have sacred power. If we would take a moment to feel the power of spirit through the natural world, we will see that all things of the earth have power and all things are connected to the great Spirit and to each other. Spirit expresses itself through the natural world.

Nature is the great teacher. She can teach you all there is to know about life, love, healing, power, and death. All we have to do is observe nature. In our modern world, we tend to overthink everything. It is difficult for us to turn off our worries and our chattering minds to be present in the circle of creation and simply be a part of everything. Spirit Walkers and witches learned about the world by simply observing it. They watch the procession of the daily sun and nightly stars. They watch the migration patterns of animals and how the birds navigate the winds. They watch the rivers flow into the oceans and how the bear hunts food for her cubs. Spirit Walkers and witches also watch the parts of nature that seem terrible to our modern-day sensibilities. They watch the wolves attack their prey and the mountain lion protect her young from predators. They watch how the act of death is necessary for life to prevail.

The natural world is beautiful and terrible all at the same time. It is up to us to see the magick of Spirit in all parts of nature. The Spirit Walker does not simply spend time in nature. The Spirit Walker *is* nature. The witch *is* nature. As we all are. But it is the duty of the Spirit Walker, the witch, and even the magician to go deep into Mother Earth and learn of her mysteries. When we reconnect to the ebb and flow of the earth's energies, our power to manifest change and heal the world becomes more powerful. Our magick comes from nature. The more we can see her beauty in our daily lives, the more we will be connected to all things on the earth and in the Universe.

Birth of Our Earth

"Anything that has mass and occupies space is matter, and accordingly includes water, all organisms, and the atmosphere, as well as minerals and rocks. Physicists recognize four states of matter; plasma (composed of ionized gas as in the sun and stars), liquids, gases, and solids." *The Changing Earth: Exploring Geology and Evolution.* James S. Monroe and Reed Wicander.

Our Earth is our home. She is our mother. She gives us food, shelter, and a place to live our lives and have our experiences. She is sacred and we should honor her to the best of our ability. Let us take a moment and travel back in time to discover how she was created and the evolution of life. In my teachings with the Lakota, rocks are called the Grandfathers. They are the oldest thing on earth and are known as spiritual record keepers. Modern science has proven this to be true. Geologist are able to discover the records of the earth and her history by looking at rocks; thanks to carbon dating and other scientific means. We owe our story here to the Grandfathers.

The beginning of the Earth actually began many billions of years after the Big Bang. Stars were formed and lived their lives for billions of years. At the time of their death, some stars went into supernova. They exploded. The elements from the remains of these dead stars were the building blocks of the solar system and our beloved Earth. The elements from the star's debris were fused together to form our sun by spinning these materials faster and faster until the sun ignited. Likewise, the planets of the solar system were created by gravity taking the stardust and forming smaller spheres around the sun. It was gravitational force that created our solar system. Our Earth began by gas, dust, and rocks forming little spheres. Once they grew in size they would be brought together through the force of gravity. The Earth was small in size and grew larger and larger as gravity would bring the elements of the stars together. This sounds much more elegant than scientists say it was. Essentially, gravity would bring rocks and elements together in a cataclysmic force of chaos. Imagine giant rocks and dust crashing into each other and causing immense nuclear reactions that caused the earth to form as a ball of rock. With this magnificent cataclysmic infusion, the core, mantle, and crust of our world was created. After the earth formed, meteorites and large rocks continued to hit the earth causing it to grow in size even further.

When the earth first formed, it was filled with volcanoes and rivers of lava. There were no oceans and the atmosphere contained no oxygen. All the water would be trapped in the interior of the young planet. This was known as the *Hadean Eon.* During this time, the crust of the earth was unstable. Partly because of the meteorites crashing into it. The other part of it was that the gravitational pull of the moon kept the liquid lava and crust from stabilizing. Eventually, the crust cooled and crystals formed. The crust formed into basalt, a dark black stone, and two-mile-high volcanoes. The atmosphere was being filled with sulphuric vapor, nitrogen, and carbon dioxide. Water was released into the atmosphere causing great storms and oceans were formed. But the oceans were not what they are today. The oceans would have looked brown with all the rocks, chemicals, and other elements floating within. This forming of the oceans contributed to the cooling of the earth's crust.

As the crust changed over millions of years, granite floated to the top of the earth through the mantel. Granit eventually replaced basalt as the earth's crust. Over millions of years, algae formed to help oxidize the atmosphere and the surface of the earth. This turned the pale grey granite into an oxidize red or rust color. Oxidation caused the basalt and granite to break down into earth making the surface appear reddish in color. This oxidation paved the way for new minerals to come into existence.

2.5 billion years ago to 542 million years ago is known as the *Proterozoic Eon.* During this time, more algae caused more oxygen to go into the atmosphere and helped the ocean become more conducive to life. During this Eon, all dry land did not look as it does today. It formed a supercontinent that a meteorologist named Alfred Wegener, called *Pangaea.* If we look at a globe or a map, we can easily see how the continents of Africa and South American could easily fit together like a giant puzzle piece. We can also see that if we move the other continents around, they could join together as well. Remember, that the shape of the continents look the way they do know because of millions of years of ocean weathering. This supercontinent was located at the equator.

During the *Neoproterozoic Eon,* the earth's atmosphere continued to cool and this resulted in the first Ice Age. This ice age lasted for millions of years and all the newly formed microbial life was almost all destroyed by the freezing temperatures. For millions of years, our world teetered between ages of ice and ages of extreme heat. These great fluctuations of temperature releases chemicals into the sea that paved the way for evolving life to be born.

In the *Ediacaran Period*, 635 million years ago, the oxygen in the atmosphere rose to accommodate life. Life evolved into newly formed creatures. Robert M. Hazen says in his book, *The Story of Earth: The First 4.5 Billion Years, From Stardust To Living Planet:*

"Elevated oxygen, in turn, has been implicated in the rise of complex multicellular life, for only with such high levels of oxygen could organisms adopt the active, energy-demanding lifestyles of jellyfish and worms."

It is during this period that the first fossils could be found. Many other ancient creatures had evolved to breath the newly oxygenated air and the stable surface.

During the *Phanerozoic Eon,* Pangaea split off into the continents that they are now and took their places on our globe. 530 million years ago, the first animals began to roam the earth. Then 360 million years ago trees and vegetation began to grow. With the evolution of the earth and its plants came the evolution of more animals that used plants as food and, in turn, other animals preyed upon those animals.

Dinosaurs walked the earth 230 million years ago. A great extinction wiped out most of the life from the previous Eon. The *Paleozoic* age was the beginning of the dinosaurs. Their body structure made it possible for them to survive and evolve from the previous age. Dinosaurs reigned for millions of years. That is until 65 million years ago an asteroid about six miles across hit what is now the Yucatan Peninsula. The massive shock wave was more powerful than several nuclear bombs. The earth was in turmoil. The impact caused tsunamis, forest fires, and the sky to turn black. The dark sky occurred because of the meteor and earth debris that was cast into the air at impact. This causes temperatures to go into freezing and the sun to be blacked out. The poor dinosaurs eventually died and became extinct.

Now that dinosaurs, the largest of the predators, were gone, other life forms were able to evolve and thrive; mammals. As mammals evolved there were several more mass extinctions. Through the process of life, death, and rebirth of species, and their evolution came the animals that we have today.

45 Million years ago saw the evolution of our first ancestral predecessors which eventually evolved into monkeys, apes, and humans. About 2.5 million years ago, the first life form that was able to use primitive tools was called *Homo habilis.* Scientists seem to have a sense of humor; this translates to Handy Man. There are a couple of scientific theories of how we, Homo sapiens, came

into being. One theory states the Homo habilis evolved further into Homo erectus, then to Homo sapien. The second theory says that there was another evolutionary life form between Homo erectus and Homo sapiens called Homo heidelbergensis. It is believed that humans, as we are now, Homo sapiens, evolved from Ethiopia and then migrated forth.

But, how was it that Earth was able to evolve as it has and eventually create life? The Earth, essentially, is in the perfect place in the Solar System to promote life. Robert M. Hazen says in his book, *The Story of Earth: The First 4.5 Billion Years, From Stardust To Living Planet:*

"Earth itself, the 'third rock from the Sun' is smack in the middle of the habitable 'Goldilocks' zone. It's close enough to the sun, and hot enough, to have relinquished significant amounts of hydrogen and helium to the outer realms of the Solar System, but it's far enough from the Sun, and cool enough, to have held onto most of its water in liquid form."

Life

"While we may be carbon-based life, composed of "long-chain" carbon molecules (carbon atoms strung together to form protein), it is the influence of three different kinds of molecules, simple molecules that exist as simple gasses, that have had the greatest influence on the history of life: oxygen, carbon dioxide, and hydrogen sulfide. Sulfur, in fact, may have been the single most important of all elements in dictating the nature and history of life on this planet." Peter Ward and Joe Kirschvink, *A New History of Life: The Radical Discoveries About the Origins of Evolution of Life on Earth.*

Life evolved on earth by molecules which created chemical reactions to create an order from itself. Essentially creating order from the chaos of random disorder of molecules. From this, molecules began to metabolize energy so that they could thrive and live. Then molecules began to duplicate or reproduce. In the theory of the evolution of life, molecules, which eventually become DNA and then cells, reproduces but does not consider itself perfect in its replication. Therefore, the molecule designs itself to change or slightly evolve. Remember, this change does not occur quickly. It is the gradual change that takes millions of years. Molecules eventually would accumulate and create amino acids and nucleotides. The molecules would grow larger and create proteins and nucleic acids. From here, they would gather even larger into something different than their environment. This "gathering" created cells. Then these cells would duplicate and then so on. The first life form that had many cells held together by membranes (multicellular) was called *Grypania*.

Our Living Earth

Our Earth is alive and changing. From her birth, 4.5 billion years ago, until now, the Earth moves and evolves. From the land to the oceans, there is movement and change. The core is one third of the Earth's mass and is 16.4% of its volume. The inner and outer cores are theorized to be made of mostly iron. The rest of the elements of the core are sulfur, silicon, oxygen, nickel and potassium. The inner core is solid while the outer core is liquid. The Mantle is made of mostly peridotite. The lithosphere is Earth's outer layer that consists of the upper mantle and the crust. The crust is an average of 35 km thick but varies depending upon the region. Mountains, of course are thicker and the sea floor is thinner.

One of the ways that the Earth is shifting and moving is through *continental drift.* Continental drift is where the plate tectonics shift and move the continents over the Earth. The first evidence of shifting plates was that when you put the continents together like a puzzle, they had similar mountains, fossils, and glacier deposits. The most notable continental puzzle piece is how South America fits into Africa. It is these two continents that also have fossils of the Mesosaurus; specifically, in Brazil and South Africa. The plates move because the lithosphere is above the asthenosphere which is much hotter and less dense than the lithosphere and heat transference occurs. To simplify, the hot upper mantle radiates immense heat to the crust and the pressure and energy causes the plates to move. When the plates are moving together this causes mountain ranges to appear as well as earthquakes and volcanoes. The core's heat comes from decaying radioactive material that releases gamma rays heating nearby rock. This heat rises to the surface and causes *thermal convection.* This is when the heat from the core rises to the lithosphere and then cools and sinks back into the mantle. This cycle repeats itself over and over. This pulls the ridges of the plates and causes them to move.

The interior of the earth is alive and constantly moving and changing. If we look deep underground into the magma (molten rock) we can see that it helps form many rock bodies from within. These rock bodies are called *plutons.* Plutons are named after the Roman God of the Underworld, Pluto. It seems that the gods are always influencing us in one way or another. All rocks are formed from magma. There are the rocks that are formed when magma crystallize below the Earth's surface and rocks that are formed when volcanic lava cools at the surface of the earth.

Earthquakes are caused by a buildup of heat, energy, and pressure along fault lines over many years caused by the movement of the continental plates. The energy released is stored in rocks. This energy is then released when the rocks are fractured and they rebound. Think of it like taking a rubber band and pulling it as far as it will go. Now pull it even further until the rubber band breaks and snaps back. I remember doing this as a kid to the rubber bands all the time. This is called the Elastic Rebound Theory. Most earthquakes take place along the edges of the plates but they can occur anywhere in the world.

The surface of the Earth is constantly changing through a process called weathering. Weathering is responsible for our soil on the ground. This happens because during the process of weathering, the large rocks are broken down into smaller and smaller pieces. There are many types of weathering. There is frost action; the repeated freezing and unfreezing of materials. Thermal expansion and contraction; the changes in the size and shape of rocks as they heat up and cool down. Animals; the daily comings and goings of animals such as digging the earth and building shelters. Chemical weathering; the decomposing of rocks through air, water, and heat. Our soil is formed by the weathering of sediment and other rocks that is infused with air, water, and other organic material.

Ceremonies For The Earth

It cannot be overstated that the earth is our Mother. In my teachings with the Lakota and Apache I was taught that we always remember Mother Earth in our ceremonies and give her thanks and healing. All life upon the earth are her children. She takes care of each of us. None of her children are held higher than the other. We, humans, tend to believe that we are superior to other life on earth simply because we talk and have the ability to create things that can both create and destroy. We must always remember that all life is equally sacred. Mother Earth cares for us by providing food and shelter upon the surface of her body. Her blood is the rivers, lakes, and oceans. The voice of Mother Earth is the song of birds, the howling of wolves, and the many different sounds made by insects and all the other animals who live upon The Mother. Our Mother Earth takes care of us. From the time we are born to the time we die and she takes us back into your sacred womb, which is the earth itself. All we have is from her.

The Sky is our Father. The sky provides us with the warmth and light of the sacred Sun and the light and dreams of The Moon. He gives us the four directional winds, each with a sacred guardian spirit. The East Wind gives us the rising sun and wisdom. The South Wind gives us healing energies and warmth. The West Wind gives us the power of dreams and self-healing. The North Wind gives us purification and community. When we look above into the night sky, we see the stars above. Each of these stars has a magick all of their own. Our Father Sky is also the home of the Thunder Beings. Mighty Beings of light who give us healing energies when we call upon them in ceremonies. Father Sky is the place where the many birds fly. Each one with sacred power of healing and spirituality. Our Father Sky gives Mother Earth the rains that help the plants grow and gives water to all life upon our her. Together Mother Earth and Father Sky maintain the balance of life, death, and rebirth. This is the sacred cycle of life.

Many times, we have to be reminded of the sacredness that is in our daily lives. Never forget that every step taken upon Mother Earth is a prayer. Every breath we take from Father Sky is a prayer. All is sacred and holy if we take the time to acknowledge it. There are times that "life" gets in the way of our connection to the earth and spirituality. Our jobs are very demanding and then we often have families, spouses, and partners that take up more time. We become so busy with everyday tasks that we forget to take a moment and connect to the energies of the earth and give back to our sacred Mother and Father. I was chatting on a Facebook group about magick and someone said, "Now that our magick has worked and we have our life goals, jobs, and families, now we have very little time for magick." I found this statement very true. We may not need to do "spells" all the time, but we still need to perform magical ceremonies. Performing ceremonies is important because by doing ceremonies and rituals it maintains our sacred connection to the Earth, the Sky, and the Universe. I always can tell when I have not done a ceremony in a while. I become more fatigued, more stressed, and more depressed. When I do not make the time for ceremony and ritual, I become disconnected from the cycles of life.

Meaning. We are born on this earth for a reason. There are some people who have known why they incarnated in this life from an early age. Many others do not find their true calling until well into adulthood. Then there are those people who do not give it much thought. All life has a meaning in the Universe. Everything from the tiniest atom to the great galaxies in deep space. Everything has a purpose and everything has a meaning. Even if you have not yet discovered what your Divine Purpose on earth is right now, we can still have meaning in our lives. As we will learn in the upcoming chapters in this book, you can be the smallest or the largest creature on earth and you have sacred meaning. When we perform ceremonies and rituals, we will begin to put sacred meaning back into our lives. I have found in my many years of doing ceremonies that eventually by connecting to the Universe and the energies of the earth sacred meaning will become a part of your life. Ceremonies always have meaning and when we connect to the sacred, we will often find purpose of our lives.

Cycles of Nature. The cycles of nature are very important. We have the daily cycles of dawn, high noon, dusk, and the night. Each part of the day has its own energies and its own blessings. Our night has the cycles of the moon. We have the growing energies of the waxing moon, the power of the full moon, the darkening energies of the waning moon, and finally, the dark of the moon with her power of mystery. And of course, we have our four seasons. The growing seasons of spring, the warmth and growth of summer, the decay of autumn, and the cold silence of winter. Even when we look at the night sky, we have the slow procession of the constellations. The cycles of nature were once very important for our survival. We had to know when to plant and reap the harvest and to know the best time to hunt and fish. Now, in our modern times, we may not be aware as much for the importance of each cycle of nature. When we use ceremonies to help us connect with the cycles of nature, we connect our own energies to those cycles. Ever wonder why there is more movement and activity with events in the spring and fall? It is because these are the times of great change in our world. Those of us who are in tune with the cycles of nature feel the ebb and flow of these energies are able to navigate our lives and the earth's energy accordingly. Sacred ceremonies help us connect to the changing energies so that we may have a closer kinship with our Mother Earth and our Father sky.

Balance and Harmony. In energy healing, we say that we need to maintain balance in order to have optimal health. We call this *homeostasis* which means to bring the body back into balance. When we are in balance, we heal much faster and are much happier. It is when things become imbalanced that sickness and disease sets in the body. This is the same when it comes to our connection with the earth. In the 21st century, people have become out of balance with nature. Pollution has caused climate change. The weather patterns all over the globe have become very extreme. Hurricanes are more and more powerful. They are hitting areas of land to where they would normally not hit. Earthquakes seem to be normal now on fault lines and rainstorms are causing great floods. This great weather phenomena are the earth's way of cleansing herself. Think of it like the immune system of Mother Earth. She is trying to purify herself of the toxins and the things that are killing her. It is vital that we reconnect with the earth and begin to heal her of the wounds that humans have caused. We must do more than recycle and reuse. We must use our sacred power, our magick, to heal our Mother Earth. If it is only one person, alone, giving healing energy to the earth then that will be a great blessing to her.

Creating Ceremony

Creating ceremonies for yourself or for a group is not as difficult as it may seem. Ceremonies are powerful and sacred ways to connect to the energies of nature so that we may have a better understanding of her as well as empower and heal ourselves. After a while, you will find that you are so connected with the earth that you can feel the full moon rising in the east and know when the last light of day has set in the west. You will feel the spirit of Mother Earth and Father Sky establish a strong spiritual connection with them. There are a few simple steps that I will give you to create your own ceremonies and rituals. In the beginning, do not worry about how "good" or how "pretty" the ceremony is. It is more important to connect to the energies of nature than how well the ceremony is done. This is a learning process and should be enjoyed. Mother Earth will not judge you for how good or simple your ritual is. She will send you loving energy simply because you are showing her how much you love her.

Intention

When creating your ceremony for the earth, the first thing you need to ask yourself is what is the ceremony for and why am I doing the ceremony? You can do seasonal earth ceremonies such as the solstices and equinoxes. These are great times to do ceremony because when we honor the changing of the seasons, we are also honoring the changes in our lives and our connection to these changing times. We can also do ceremonies for the full and dark moons. If you choose, some Spirit Walkers and witches do daily ceremonies. The rising sun is a wonderful time for ceremony. The rising sun is new beginnings, the start of new intentions and purpose, as well as a lot of healing energy. One metaphor is to think of the returning light of the sun as the healing energy that dispels the darkness. For our purpose with this book we will perform a ceremony to heal the earth.

Sacred Tools

After you have decided on your purpose for the ritual, you will need to gather your sacred tools. You may use drums, rattles, crystals, herbs, or any other item that speaks to you. The only thing that is a "must" is that all your items you use in ceremony must be as natural as possible. If we are sending healing energy to the earth, it makes little sense to do so with unnatural items. There is no rule of what kind of tools you must have for Spirit Walking and witchcraft. I, personally, like bringing my smudging tools, drum, and sacred herbs. Although, there have been many times that I have gone out in nature and used a stick and some rocks I found to send energy. The only tool you MUST have is you! For our ceremony now, we will bring sage and a bowl to place it in (abalone shell works well), a drum or rattle, water, and a bowl to hold the water.

Calling the energies

When we are calling the energies, we are doing far more than just calling energy. We are calling the spirits of the four directions, Mother Earth and Father Sky, the ancestors, and the spirits of the cosmos such as the sun, moon, stars, and planets. We are also calling animal spirits to help us. We will talk more about animal spirits later in this book. There are many ways to call the energies and spirit into your ceremony. In Lakota, we sing sacred songs to each of these spirits and ask them to help us. In other traditions, you may reach out with your heart to the spirits and, with sincerity and love, ask them to come to your ceremony and give of themselves to help you perform your magick. The important thing to do when calling the energies is to connect to each of them with your heart. Take a moment to really feel them. This is what true magick looks like. We tune in and feel the spirit we are calling forth. The more you work with the spirits listed here, the more you will be able to feel their energies and the easier it is to call them into your ceremony. Each time I call a spirit, I call them by name and then tell them the reason I am calling upon them. Then I ask them to help me with the purpose of the ceremony.

Focus the Energy

Once I have called the energies and spirits into my ceremony, I will gather the energy in my body or a sacred tool. Then I will visualize the outcome I would like to have. For our ceremony now, I will visualize Mother Earth healed from her wounds. I will see her free of pollution: clean water, clear skies, soil that is pure and healthy, and all life on earth in harmony with the earth's life cycles.

Releasing the Energies

There are several different ways you can release the energies that your ceremony has accumulated. You can breathe the energies into your body and release them through your hands towards your target. You can use one of your sacred tools to absorb the energy and send it through the focused Will towards your target. You can also ask the spirits that you have summoned to take the energy towards the target. For example, if I called Bear into my ceremony for healing, I can ask Bear to take the healing energy to the person the ceremony is for.

Thanks and Offerings

Once you have completed the main part of your ceremony, you will need to thank all the spirits and energies that you have called. You can be very elaborate or simple with your thank you. You can also sing a song of thanks. At this point the spirits will depart or stay around. I never banish or ask them to leave. These spirits are our honored guests and they have done us a great service by lending their powers to us. They may stay if they wish. You will also need to give them an offering of some kind. Being in the United States, I prefer to give the spirits of nature tobacco, but you can use any herbs, food, wine, or water to give offerings. Just remember anything you leave outside for the spirits should be all natural.

Follow Through

Always have follow through on all ceremonies and rituals you perform. If you are looking for a job, go out and look for a job, if you are in need of healing then make sure you are doing things that will aide in healing. If you are doing ceremony to heal the earth, make sure you are doing things that will help heal her such as recycling, reusing, and cleaning up areas you can such as parks and other natural places.

Ceremony To Heal the Earth

Items needed:

Drum or rattle, sage and vessel, lighter, water, bowl, small blanket or rug.

Intent and purpose:

To heal the earth.

1. Gather your ceremony items and go out into a place in nature. For this ceremony, the further away from humans the better.
2. Place your blanket or rug down on the ground. Place all of your tools on the blanket or rug and sit down directly upon the earth. If you are unable to sit upon the earth you can bring a camping folding chair.
3. Spend a few moments connecting with nature. Feel the wind on your body. Listen to the wild life nearby. Feel the warmth of the sun. Feel the ground beneath you. Take deep breaths of the air.
4. State out loud your intent to heal the earth. You can use your own words or say, **"I come on this sacred day to send healing energy to my Mother the Earth."**
5. Connect with the four directions, Mother Earth, Father

Sky, the ancestors and the celestial energies. Call them into your ceremony. Again, you can speak with your heart or say, **"I call to you ancestors. I seek to heal the earth and I ask that you lend me your energies. I call to you Mother Earth and Father Sky. I come to give you, Mother, healing energy. I call to the four winds. East, South, West, and North. I ask that you join me in healing Mother Earth. To the celestials I call upon you to assist me in healing our Mother Earth. Sun, moon, stars and all planets above. I ask that you send your energies here to heal our Mother."**

6. Once you feel the energies have gathered to your ceremony space you must direct the energies. Take the water and pour it into the bowl. Now direct the energies of healing into the bowl. You can visualize the energies as different colors of light going into the bowl of water directly or you can summon the energies into your own body and direct the energies into the bowl of water through your hands. Also, you may add your own energies as well.

7. When you feel the bowl of water is full of energy say, **"Mother Earth please accept these healing energies I give to you now."** Pour the bowl of healing water on the ground. Visualize the healing energy going to the parts of the earth that need the most healing.

8. Thank all the spirits you have called. Explain to them in your own words that they are welcome to stay but you understand if they have to go back to where they came.

9. Remember to keep the spirit of healing Mother Earth every day. Do what you can to protect her from harm and destruction. Be a model for others and inspire them to heal our Mother as well.

This ceremony is only a quick ritual to get you going. As long as you keep the main points, you can change and adapt the ceremony for your own purposes. As long as you maintain the purpose of healing, connection, and love of nature and the Universe your ceremonies will be great.

Nature Healing

Being outside in nature is one of the best sources of healing. We are meant to be outside, not observing nature, but being a part of it. When humans first came into existence, we were part of the earth and its environmental cycles. Our five senses developed to tell our brains and our bodies what was happening around us. Our sense of smell is very powerful. Scientists have discovered that our sense of smell affects our minds in such a way that it brings memories back to us. We harmonized with the landscapes and the seasons. We become in tune with the ebb and flow of natural energies. The sun guided our way by day and the moon sang us to sleep by night. We also looked to the living things as a part of our Universe. Plants and trees had voices and medicine while animals, birds, and fish had much wisdom to teach us.

With the invention of modern technology, most of us have forgotten about the wisdom of nature and even have learned to fear it. In the 21st Century, many of us no longer work the land as we used to or go hunting in the forest for our food. We no longer give gratitude and honor the plants and animals that have been sacrificed for our well-being and nourishment. We are disconnected from the natural cycles of life, death, and rebirth. Bugs and animals are strange and even scary to us because we do not understand them. Technology has turned our focus inward to a smart phone and no longer to the paths that go deep into the forests.

Technology, in itself, is not bad. I am typing on this computer to bring my experience and teachings to you, the internet is where we learn and share information, and hospitals have lifesaving equipment that have saved thousands of lives. Like with anything, technology can be abused and take our focus of our lives. As pagans, witches, and Spirit Workers, we must learn to hear nature speak to us. Nature has so much wisdom and medicine to offer. We only have to listen. But how do we do that? It is very easy. All you have to do is put down your phone and walk outside. Don't stop. Keep walking to the park, the forest, the mountain, the lake, the beach, or anywhere close to you that is nature. Yes, you may drive. We need technology to help us get to nature sometimes.

The natural world is filled with spirits and animal helpers. The trees have spirits. Each blade of grass and each plant has a spirit. Along with this, the animals have profound wisdom and healing to show us. All we have to do to receive these gifts is to listen to the song of nature. Nature is both quiet and loud, but her language is all her own. In ages past, we could communicate with Nature very easily, but in our modern times we have lost the ability to hear this sacred language. The language and songs of nature helps us heal and keeps us in balance with our environment and the Universe. When we are disconnected from nature disharmony sets in which leads to disease and unhappiness. If you look around you or simply read the news you will see how many people and countries are out of balance with nature. We destroy forests and other precious lands to build buildings and parking lots. Chemicals in the land is causing destruction and disease. In energy healing we say that your body and the land are connected.

It is time for us to reconnect with the magick of the land. In order to do this, we simply have to find a little bit of nature and go for a walk. By walking in nature, we are re-establishing our relationship with the outside world. Walking in nature is one of the best healing techniques I have found. Susan S. Scott says in her book *Healing With Nature:*

"Walking therapy...could be practiced in nature. What was encountered would become part of the healing process. The

Shape of a tree, or the weather, or the meow of a cat on the sidewalk, or the sweat on one's brow-all of these moments were part of walking therapy. Without walls, nature and the relationship between client and therapists would be what held meaning and contained the experience."

Healers know that nature is magical and provides much wisdom and insight. When we connect to the energies of nature, we find balance and wholeness. Once this is achieved, we are able to connect with the earth and establish relationships with the trees, plants, and animals. One of the most powerful techniques I learned was what is sometimes called the *Spirit Walk*. With this technique you will reconnect with nature and learn to hear the sacred voices of the earth. The Spirit Walk is the foundation of the rest of the magick found in this book. It is simple, yet very powerful.

The Spirit Walk

1. Go to the natural world. You can go to a forest, beach, desert, park, or prairie. If possible, try to do this without the distraction of several people. However, you can do this with your magical group or another like-minded friend.
2. Take a few deep breaths and center yourself in this natural space. Take a moment and listen to the sounds of nature. Listen to the breeze in the tree or the waves of the ocean and the songs of the animals nearby. Smell the natural scents.
3. Continue to take long deep breaths and allow these breaths to place you into a light trance.
4. Now, breathe in the life force of the earth through your feet.
5. Breathe in the life force the nature that is all around you.
6. Breathe in the sounds of the animals and the winds.

7. Allow these energies to fill your body with this healing life force of nature.
8. As you continue breathing, allow your eyes to slightly get heavy. Go into trance.
9. Have the sacred intention to connect with the earth. Begin walking through nature. Your squinted eyes may allow you to see the aura of the plants and animals. Become aware of the energies that nature is sending out.
10. Walk through nature as long as you like. When you are finished, give gratitude for the earth and the lessons you have learned today. Give an offering of tobacco or simply some of your personal energy.
11. Journal your experiences.

Chapter 2

The Otherworld

There is an energetic and mystical world that resides next to our own. This magical place is spoken of in myths and legends of the Celtic and Northern European people. Sometimes it is called Elfheim or Elfland. In the Middle Ages, the term "elf" came to mean any spirit of nature that was neither angel nor demon. It is also sometimes referred to as Faeryland or simply *Faery*. Meaning, this is the land of the Fey. For many magical people, we simply call this wondrous place the Otherworld. In some spiritual traditions, such as the Celtic tradition, the Otherworld encompasses all of the shamanic three worlds within one world of spirit. In Celtic mythology, the Otherworld contains the land of the dead which is a place of beauty and feasting. It also contains the realms of the gods and other beings that involve themselves with human affairs from time to time. There is a wonderful theory in quantum physics that says there are many other worlds much like our own but they reside in other planes of existence. In quantum physics, It is believed that our universe is not alone in the vastness of creation. There is the theory of the *multiverse*. This is the theory that there are many other universes besides our own. In fact, there could be countless. Some universes could perhaps exist in another dimension. In the theory of other dimensions, the fourth dimension is Time and the fifth dimensions is what we humans consider the world of Spirit or the Otherworld. With this hypothesis, another universe could exist side by side to ours.

The Otherworld is the world of elves, faeries, nature spirits, spirit animals, and many other spiritual beings that have an effect on the physical plane. In his book *The Fairy-Faith in Celtic Countries*, W.Y. Evans-Wentz says:

"...this western Otherworld, if it is what we believe it to be-a poetical picture of the great subjective world-cannot be the realm of any one race of invisible beings to the exclusion of another. In it all alike-gods, Tuatha De Danann, fairies, demons, shades, and every sort of disembodied spirits-find their appropriate abode; for though it seems to surround and interpenetrate this planet even as the X-rays interpenetrate matter, it can have no other limits than of the Universe itself."

When one enters the Otherworld, it is sometimes described as bright and shining or the glowing of starlight. This is because the Otherworld glows with the radiance of the energetic force of life and creation. In her book *Celtic Myth and Religion: A Study of Traditional Belief, with Newly Translated Prayers, Poems and Songs,* Sharon Paice MacLeod says, "The Celtic Otherworld itself was described as a realm of great beauty and power, an almost dreamlike place where colors, sounds, and experiences were intensified". As we know, the physical plane is formed by the flowing of energies from the spiritual plane down to the astral. Once these energies are in the astral plane they begin to form in a more tangible way. In magical thought, the astral plane is the formation stage of creation. From there, the energies flow into the etheric plane to be finalized by the life-giving energies that are found here. Then, the physical plane is formed from culmination of these forces. The Otherworld can be seen as the final intercessory between the worlds of spirit and the world of the physical. Picture it this way, the Otherworld is the realm between formation of the astral plane and finalization of the physical plane. This is also why the landscape looks almost identical to the physical landscape but it shines with light. It contains the final energetic form to all life and matter in the Universe. I have found that the beings who live in the Otherworld, such as Elves, Faeries, and Dragons help the energies of life and creation flow into the physical plane. There is a very powerful magical link between the land and the Otherworld because of this. The Otherworld beings have the ability to guide the life force, that flows to them from Spirit, through their world and into the physical plane. These beings are closely related to nature and the cycles of birth, growth, decay, and death.

Time runs very differently in the Otherworld. There are many tales of how someone found themselves in the world of Faery and then returned to the mortal land hundreds of years later. In the poem, *The Voyage of Bran,* Bran goes on a voyage into the Otherworld by boat with many men. He visits many Otherworldly islands on his adventure. One such island is the Isle of Joy where everyone cannot stop laughing. One man is entranced by this joy and is left behind. Then they come to the Isle of Women, where once again, the men are enchanted by the Otherworldly women and they stay there for what they thought was one year. When Bran returns to his homeland, one of his men gets off his horse. When his feet touch the physical earth, he immediately turns to dust. This clearly shows that Bran and his men have been gone many years. So many that their physical bodies should have turned to dust. Time also runs very slowly as well. When you enter the Otherworld, you may be there for hours or many days to discover that you were only there for a few minutes. There have been many times my circle and I have opened the veil between this world and the Otherworld for magical rites and spent what we thought was hours performing magick; working with the elves and fey, and many other beings, only to discover that mere minutes had past. In the Otherworld, time is neither here nor there. What I mean is that when it comes to the Otherworld all things past, present, and future are all happening at once. In essence, all that ever was and all that ever will be flows in constant motion. This is one of the reasons why we are able to use oracles to divine into the past, present, and future. Also, time in our physical world must be constant in order to maintain balance. It is true, that time is a man-made construct, but the earth goes around the sun the same way and the moon orbits the earth in constant motion. All of these things maintain the balance of the physical world. However, in the Otherworld, time does not need to flow the same way. The spirit worlds are not constrained by physical laws so, therefore, the energies may flow as they will, or how the Otherworldly beings direct them to do so.

Throughout the lore of the Celts, there are tales of the Otherworld and our world overlapping. There are tales of magick castles, Faery Queens who find mortal lovers, humans who accidentally slip into the Otherworld, and people who have seen elvish and faery beings wandering through the green wood. One of the more famous of the Faery ballads is Thomas the Rhymer. Thomas meets the Queen of Elfland and goes away with her and does not return to the mortal world for seven years. The Queen of the Fey showed Thomas many marvelous things, one of them was the three roads. One of the roads led to Hell, the other to Heaven, and the third to Elfland. Thomas is not just a character in a ballad, he is based on an actual historical figure who lived in the 13th Century. He was said to have the gift of prophecy. Was this a magical power given to him by the Queen of the Faeries? Or perhaps she was attracted to him because he naturally possessed this Otherworldly power.

There are many tales of people finding mysterious Otherworld castles or fortresses. One of these castles is The Spiral Castle that is the home of the goddess, Arianrhod. This castle continues to spiral in a circle making it difficult for the traveler to enter. Once the castle was found, perhaps the goddess would grant you the powers of inspiration as well as other magical tools. In the Traditional Witchcraft that I was initiated in, the Spiral Castle could only be entered in the Otherworld on the night of the full Moon. The easiest way to find it was on the night of the full moon, trace the path of the moon upon the ocean or large body of water. On the watery horizon, under the moon, would be the spiraling castle. Then you may travel upon the moon path in spirit.

The Otherworld contains many different wondrous places. This was a place of joy, happiness, and mystery. There were many different "lands" in the Otherworld. Some of the names were The Land of Youth, The Land of Honey, The Land of Women, The Land of Mists, The Land of Joy, and so on. Each of these lands was a place of beauty, music, and great happiness. Some of these places were thought to be islands in the Otherworld. In *The Voyage of Bran,* Bran, who is the king, sets out on an Otherworldly voyage after he dreams of a beautiful woman who tells him of the Isle of Women. When Bran and his men arrive at the Isle of Women, the inhabitants of the island use their magical powers to bring the men to their sacred island. There, they are well fed and cared for. Every need and enjoyment are met by the beautiful women upon the island. In Arthurian legend, King Arthur is mortally wounded in the Battle of Camlann and is taken by this sister, Morgan La Fey, to the Isle of Avalon for healing. The Isle of Avalon, translated as the Island of Apples, is said to be a magical place of healing that is governed by Morgan Ley Fey and her nine sisters.

There are many animals that are sacred to the Otherworld. In myth, many different types of animals may appear to someone traveling in the woods. Many times, the animals of the Otherworld are white. There are many tales of someone finding a mysterious white animal that leads them to the world of Faery. In the Lakota tradition, White Buffalo Calf Woman first appears as a white buffalo calf from the Spirit World to two scouts. She tells them to prepare for her arrival in the tribe. She then gives them the sacred pipe in order for them to pray to the creator. In Celtic myth, the White Stag is an animal of the Faeries. It often appears to lead the wanderer deep into the woods in order to pass through the veil into the Otherworld.

Otherworldly Tools

In the Traditional Witchcraft that I was taught, there are four sacred tools of the Otherworld that correspond to the four portals of the magical circle or compass. Let me begin with explaining the four portals. In many modern witchcraft circles, we have the four directions that correspond with the four elements. In the east we have the element of air and new beginnings, the south the element of fire and highest manifestation, the west the element of water and waning of energy, and north the element of earth and the silence or quietness of energy. In my traditional craft, each of the elements blend into each other to create the cross quarters of North East, South East, South West, and North West. The traditional witch can then open up a portal to each of the cross quarters. The North East portal is the portal of Birth/ Re-birth. On the pagan wheel of the year it corresponds to Imbolc. The South East portal is the portal of Fate/ Destiny and corresponds to Beltaine. The South West is the portal of Mystery and corresponds to Lughnasadh. The North West is the portal of Death and corresponds to Samhain. In each of the portals there is a magical tool of the Otherworld. The North East portal contains the Sword, the South East portal contains the Spear, the South West portal contains the Cauldron, and the North West portal contains the Stone. For clarity, let us look at the magical circle with both the quarters and cross quarters.

North East- Birth/ Rebirth, Imbolc, Sword
East- Youth, Ostara, Athame
South East- Fate/ Destiny, Beltaine, Staff or Spear
South- Adulthood, Litha, Wand
South West- Mystery, Lughnasadh, Cauldron
West- Maturity, Mabon, Chalice
North West- Death, Samhain, Stone
North- Afterlife, Yule, Pentacle

As you can see, the quarters of the compass are the elemental energies that are flowing *toward* the circle in order to aid the witch in manifestation upon the physical plane while the cross quarter of the circle are the energies of change that are flowing *toward* the Otherworld. Each portal has a great mystery of the Otherworld that each person should work with and discover all on their own. After all a good teacher guides the student to places of power but the student must travel to them all on their own.

The Traditional Craft I was initiated into came to us from Wales so I will conjecture that the Four Otherworldly Tools that is in our tradition is somewhat based on the Four Otherworldly Tools found in Celtic mythology. But what exactly are the tools of the Otherworld and what is their purpose to us? The tools, in essence, are the physical manifestation of Otherworld energies that have a specific purpose. As we have learned, the Otherworld brings the energies of regeneration and life force to the physical plane. At certain times, these energies are needed to manifest as a magical tool in order for the witch or magician to manifest its power for the greater good of both worlds.

The Sword

The Sword is the magical tool that is associated with the portal of Birth/ Rebirth. It is the tool that cuts the physical umbilical cord at birth as well as the energetic cord that attaches the spirit of the human child to the Spirit World. It has the power to direct the energies of the Otherworld for greater magical purposes and defence if needed. In Celtic myth, it is associated with the Sword of Nuado. It was believed that this tool of the Otherworld always got its intended victim in battle.

The Spear

The Spear is the tool that is associated with the portal of Fate/ Destiny. It is the tool that "spears" the desire of the witch or magician. It is also the tool that signifies a position of leadership as a spiritual as well as physical warrior. The Spear helps the witch or magician focus their magical intent in order to obtain what they are destined for. Even though we are destined for greatness, it is our job to go out and get it. In Celtic mythology, it is associated with the Spear of Lugh. It is believed that this tool had the power to win battles and protect its wielder from harm.

The Cauldron

The Cauldron is the tool associated with the portal of Mystery. It is the tool that provides healing and nourishment. It is also the tool that is used as a portal to the Otherworld allowing spirits to come forth from the vessel when conjured for acts of magick. The witch or magician could travel in spirit form into the cauldron into the Otherworld. In Celtic mythology, it is the Cauldron of the Dagda. It is believed that this tool has the power to grant food to everyone and no one would be left hungry.

The Stone

The Stone is the tool associated with the portal of Death. It is the tool is used to contain the spirits of the dead when they are conjured by the witch or magician. It is also the tool that is used to bind hostile spirits to the grave to prevent them from doing harm. In Celtic mythology it is associated with the Stone of Fal. It is believed that this tool would scream under the feet of the true king.

Blessings of the Otherworld

The Otherworld energies are needed for the wellbeing, fertility, and growth of our physical world. Without these life-giving energies, the land will become desolate and will not produce energies needed for the growth and vitality of plants, animals, and the land itself. The earth will become a wasteland. It is vital that the Otherworld continue its flow of life force to us.

The Otherworld also needs our energies in return. Just as we know to give offerings and energies to the gods and ancestors, it is important the we give back energy to the Otherworld in return. It is important that we are in right relationship with the Otherworld and Otherworld beings. The Otherworld gives restorative energies to our physical world freely as long as we maintain proper energy exchange. The energy exchange needed to maintain balance is, essentially, to return the honor and respect back to the Otherworld that is given to us. When Otherworld beings such as Elves, Faeries, Nature Spirits, and Dragons give us healings and blessings, we must show them honor and respect. This keeps the flow of healing energy constantly going. When humans become greedy with the land, and its blessings, we block the restorative powers of the Otherworld and the energies become stagnant causing the land to become a wasteland. When we give back to the spirits of the land and the Otherworld through seasonal rites, offerings, and energy exchange our world and the Otherworld remain in harmony.

Let us take a moment and look at the Grail Mythos from England. In the story there is a King who had been wounded in the thigh/genitals. Because the king is energetically connected to the land, whatever happens to the king happens to the kingdom. Therefore, because the king cannot reproduce neither can the land produce food. The Grail King and his maidens live in a place called The Grail Castle that appears and disappears at will. The Grail Castle is between this world and the Otherworld. One day a young knight, named Parzival, finds the poor king fishing and is invited back to the castle. During his stay, he sees beautiful maidens carrying the sacred grail. Because of his lack of experience and foolishness, he does not realize he should ask certain questions to break the enchantment of the castle. The next morning, he leaves the castle and it disappears. After many years of both physical and spiritual trials, he is spiritually evolved enough to return to the castle and ask the right questions to the grail king. The correct question is "Who is served by the Grail?" When this happens, the spell is broken and the Grail King is healed by the grail and Parzival becomes the grail king, but this time, he has a spiritual experience and wisdom and needs not to be wounded to discover enlightenment. Joseph Campbell says in his book *Romance of the Grail: The Magical Mystery of Arthurian Myth:*

> "One of the characters of an enchantment is that there are people all around who know the rules of the enchantment. These are the people of the Grail Castle community. They know what the curse is and how it works, but they can't dispel it. The only way the enchantment can be broken is by some naive person doing the thing that has to be done unintentionally, out of his true nature."

The grail, in this story, is another version of a magical tool from the Otherworld known as the Cauldron of Plenty. This cauldron never empties of food, drink, or medicine and is a gift of Otherworldly beings to those who are worthy of its magick. This vessel is the manifestation of the intrinsic power of the earth that is creating life and regenerating life at the same time. The force that makes the plants grow and gives energy to all beings upon the earth to live. The trick is that not just anyone may use the magick of the grail/cauldron. It can only be wielded by someone who has overcome earthly selfishness and wants to heal others, not for glory or ego, but because it is the right thing to do. There is no reward in doing the right thing. We do it just because it is right. This is how you are able to use tools and magical items from the Otherworld.

The Land of Elves and Faeries

There are many magical places to travel to in the Otherworld. In Nordic myth, there is the land of the Elves called *Ljusalfheim.* In the lore, it is said to be just near Asgard, the world of the Asatru gods in the Upperworld. I have found, through my experience and work with the Elves, that Ljossalfheim, sometimes called Elfheim or Alfheim, is actually the "upper" part of Middle Earth. In the cosmology of the northern Europeans, the lore and myths often place Asgard, Lyossalfheim, and Vanaheim in the Upperworld; Muspelheim (world of fire), Midgard, and Jotunheim, in the Midworld; and Svartalheim, Helheim, and Niflheim (world of ice) in the Underworld. If we look at the creation myths, it says that Muspelheim existed and Niflheim existed and when they came together, their union created the nine worlds. If we translate these two worlds to into physics, then Muspelheim can be seen as the world of cosmic forces such as gamma rays, radio waves, and light and Niflheim into dark energy, dark matter, and antimatter. If we use this theory then Muspelheim can be seen as the Big Bang of creation and certainly has the energies of the Source of all creation. So, I believe that Muspelheim is above Asgard in the Upperworld and Ljusalfheim is in the Midworld. I also have come to believe that the nine worlds are not as cut and dry as you might think. I think that the nine words are more of a spiral rather than three in the upperworld, three in the Midworld, and three in the underworld. So I think it makes more sense to have Muspelheim beginning in the upperworld at the very top, then Asgard, Vanaheim, then the Midworld being Ljossalfheim, Midgard, Jotunheim, then underworld with Svartalheim, Helheim, and Niflheim at the very bottom of the Universe. My other reasoning for placement Ljusalfheim in the Midworld is because the world of the elves is a world of nature and is very close to our own. The elves often interact with humans and we are only separated by an energetic veil that can be easily crossed with magick.

Ljusalfheim is a beautiful world of light and magick. It is a place of nature that shines with power and lifeforce. The land itself is very similar to our own as well as the Faery Otherworld.

It seems to have almost the same qualities as the Otherworld. Perhaps it is one and the same. Whenever you cross the veil into Ljusalfheim it seems as though it is the energetic counterpart of the physical world. For instance, if you live near mountains then the Elf world will have mountains. If you live in the grassy plains, then the Elf world will have grassy plains. Another attribute to this world is that it can change and alter at will. This is because, even though it is close to the physical plane, it is still made up of energy. The Elves have a monarchy with kings, queens, and royal nights as well as villagers. You can find glistening castles and strongholds as well as quaint elf villages, towns, and cities. Sometimes the structures in Ljusalfheim appear to be glass or crystal. If you find yourself deep in the Elvish forests, mountains, or other natural landscape be prepared for many other wondrous creatures other than the elves. Freyr, the Nordic god of fertility, rules this magical world. It was given to him as an infant as a "teething" gift. Meaning a gift for the god when he had his first tooth. This is a magical land and anything can happen, especially magick.

The Land of the Faeries is, perhaps, the most famous of all of the places in the Otherworld. Like the Otherworld itself, the land of the fey is not one thing you can describe eloquently enough in one book. Celtic lore speaks of Land of Faery in many different ways. Often it is described as a place that is bright and shining with beauty and magick. Many tales speak of enchanted castles and magical forests that are constantly shifting and changing because of the nature of the magick in that realm. This is a place of enchantment, glamour, and magick. I have come to believe that the world of Faerie is so magical because it is in the Otherworldly realm that is in between the energetic formation of the creation and the physical realm itself. Faeryland finds itself in between the world of spirit and the regenerative energies of the land.

Another aspect of the Otherworld is The Land of Wild

Nature. This part of the Otherworld is very close to our own physical world and is a place of chthonic primal energies. To the ancient Northern European people, the land of the giants was beyond the hedge in the dark and mysterious forests that held many dangers and life-threatening animals. This place was an intercessory between the physical world and the Otherworld. This is the land of wild storms of rain, hail, or snow and winds that are a force to be reckoned with. This is also the land of giant waves that destroy cities upon the shore and earthquakes that destroyed cities. This is the world of the natural forces of nature that create and destroy life. Wild nature has no right or wrong nor good or bad. It simply creates and destroys with the cycles of the seasons and the movements of weather patterns upon the earth. This world wields powerful forces of nature that are uncontained and free to use its full magick upon the Universe.

The Land of Wild Nature is the land of the giants. This world is very close to the physical plane. For within the ancient forests are magnificent beasts that are some of the fiercest predators in the shamanic worlds. In Nordic Myth, this land is called Jotunheim, or the land of the giants. In his book *The Pathwalkers Guide To The Nine Worlds,* Raven Kaldera says this about Jotunheim, "It is the land that is both forbidding and exhilarating, beautiful and dangerous. As is appropriate for Giant-Home, everything grows larger there. Trees are enormous, forests thick and towering, animals' eminence and fierce." There are many cities, forts, castles, and great halls where the giants live. When traveling to Jotunheim, you should leave an offering of some kind for the giant folk to allow you safe passage in this land. They are very fond of ale, mead, and hard liquor. Meat offerings will work as well. This land is harsher than the other worlds in the nine worlds and it is better if you have the giants on your side. Giving offerings shows good faith and they may allow you to pass through. The benefits of journeying to this land is that it contains many magical giants who are proficient in magick, oracle work, sorcery, and healing. You will definitely need to bring an offering to these magical beings. They tend to be cranky and are not fond of strangers. They may even ask for you to prove your worth to them before they help you magically or teach you their secrets.

Finding The Otherworld

Finding the Otherworld can be as simple as wandering through the veil between words on accident and as complicated as using advanced magical practices to find your way through the portal between this world and the Otherworld. The most common way that people may stumble into the Otherworld is by finding *between places*. That is, any place that is in between two things or between two opposites is an entryway into a magical place. Places like doors and window frames are common entrances to the Otherworld because it is neither inside nor outside. Another example of in between is he shore line of an ocean or lake because it is neither in the water nor on dry land. In Celtic lore, sacred wells are a marvelous place to find the Otherworld. The water from wells are said to flow from the healing and rejuvenating powers of the Otherworld. The earth itself has lifegiving energies beneath the surface and the water from under the earth contains this magical energy. They are also places that are in between. They are both in the physical world and the Otherworld. They are both above the earth and below the earth. There are dates and times that are in between as well. Dawn and dusk are in between times because they are neither day nor night. For the solar year, the greatest in between days are Beltaine and Samhain because they are in between the Celtic Summer and Winter times. Interestingly enough, it is said that the season and time of day is the opposite in the Otherworld than it is here in our world. So, therefor, when the veil was thin for us between the days of Summer and Winter the veil was thin in the Otherworld between their days between Winter and Summer and vice versa;

an interesting thing to note, I think.

Beyond the Hedge

For many people hundreds of years ago, living in a small town or village kept you safe from the unknown world. The village had the protection of many people, public buildings, and residences. There was the safety within the fire light spaces that kept the shadows of the unknown at bay. For many European villages, the only thing that separated them from the dark forest was a hedge. For beyond the hedge was the dark forests that contained wild animals, bandits, thieves, and evil spirits. The hedge was considered the boundary between this world and the world of the spirits. The foreboding forest was an intersection between our world and the land of the giants, trolls, elves, faeries and many other things. It was also the intercessory between us and the Otherworld which, not only contained the woodland spirits, but also contained monsters that brought disease and death. The cunning man, witch, and Spirit Walker would usually live near the hedge because they preferred to live in between the worlds. To go beyond the hedge was to go into the deep forests of dangerous spirits. Eric de Vries in his book *Hedge-Rider* says, "The hedge is the Boundary, separating the two and was thus an 'in-between' place. All this is symbolic of Middle-Earth and the Otherworld, as well as culture and the wild."

Journey to the Otherworld

The Otherworld has much magick and wisdom to offer. By journeying to the Otherworld, we can reclaim the sacredness of our lives. We begin to understand our greater purpose on earth and how we can help and heal others. There is much healing that comes from the earth. Remember, from our point of view, this is a world that is the most balanced, and, so, it is a place that can balance our energy and bring us back to wholeness and health. The land, seas, and skies give us life force that is healing. We can learn to work with the nature spirits of the earth. In Native American cosmology, all beings from animals to plants to minerals are our teachers. Every plant and mineral have their "medicine". By working with nature spirits, they can teach us how to find health and happiness through the balance of creation.

The Otherworld is home to our sacred animal teachers and helpers. Each animal has a divine place in the Universe. By observing them and working with them in spirit they have many things to teach us about ourselves and the world around us. Each animal has a unique gift of healing. When we journey to the Otherworld, we will learn their magical gifts and their place in the Universe. They can also teach us how to act on their behalf in the physical plane. As they have a voice for us in the astral worlds, we must have a voice for them in the physical. The Otherworld is also home to Elves, Faeries, Dwarves, and many other beings. These beings can help us develop our magick and our healing skills. Elves and Faeries are known for their skills in crafts and arts and can teach us many new things. Dwarves are known for their knowledge in minerals and the caves of the earth. The spirits of the earth can help us find direction in our own lives and find greater purpose.

Astral Projection and Shamanic Journeying

There has been a lot said over the years about astral projecting and shamanic journeying. Astral projection is another world for shamanic journeying. So, you can use them interchangeably. Many people will say that it takes an adept to be able to leave your body in spirit and that you cannot achieve this magical technique without years of study. I disagree. Granted, I do not recommend astral projection and journeying if you have little to no magical experience but as long as you have your rudimentary basics you can apply this technique very easily. In shamanistic cultures, in order to learn the ways of the Spirit Walker one of the very first things you learn to do is leave your body is spirit. The Lakota Spiritual Leader Wallace Black Elk spoke of leaving his body when he was very young during a sickness and conversing with the spirits. The spirits are the ones who really teach us. Books such as this is a great starting point, but it is the power and wisdom of the spirits who help us become powerful witches and Spirit Walkers.

Do not worry about getting lost in the spirit worlds or never finding your body again. Stories like this are nothing more than fear based and, honestly, gatekeeping. We astral project every single day sometimes without knowing it. We project when we dream and when we daydream. Have you ever been thinking about someone so hard that you could smell the room they were in or you knew exactly what clothes they were wearing? You were astral projecting. Also, it is very common to be aware of the Otherworld and your physical body at the same time. This is because part of your consciousness is still in your physical body. It has to be. Otherwise you would not be alive. This is very useful as well. It will help you in way-taming as well as treating sick clients who come to you for energy healing. You can send your astral body out and get information and summon healing energy from the Otherworld while you are administering healing to your client. Being able to be aware of your physical body while traveling in spirit is a gift.

Astral Exercise #1

1. It may be helpful to play a shamanic drumming recording. If you have someone to drum for you all the better. The drumming should be very light, but audible enough to hear comfortably. If you are using a drum or having someone drum for you, have them beat at a moderately quick pace. If for some reason you cannot get a recording of shamanic drumming, don't worry. It is not necessary to have a shamanic drum beat to astral project.

2. Sit or lie in a comfortable position. Make sure your back is as straight as possible.
3. Close your eyes and take a few deep breaths.
4. Relax your body as best you can. Begin with your feet. Tell them to relax and release all tension. Then move up to your calf. Tell them to relax and release all tension. Go up to the thighs, glutes, back, belly, chest, shoulders, arms, hands, neck, and head in turn, telling them all to relax and release all stress and tension.
5. Now, visualize yourself getting up and walking around. Remember, this is done entirely with your imagination. Try not to move your physical body at all.
6. Walk around the room you are in and look at the furniture, walls, shelves. Look at yourself. See yourself lying (or sitting) down.
7. When you are ready, see yourself walk over to your physical body and sit or lie back into yourself. When you are close to your body this will most often happen automatically.

Astral Exercise #2

1. Play your shamanic drumming recording if you have one as per the previous exercise.
2. Sit or lie in a comfortable position. Make sure your back is as straight as possible.
3. Close your eyes and take a few deep breaths.
4. Relax your body as best you can. Begin with your feet. Tell them to relax and release all tension. Then move up to your calf. Tell them to relax and release all tension. Go up to the thighs, glutes, back, belly, chest, shoulders, arms, hands, neck, and head in turn, telling them all to relax and release all stress and tension.
5. Imagine yourself getting up and walking around. Remember, this is done entirely with your imagination.

Try not to move your physical body at all.

6. At this point, see a door or gateway in front of you. Know that the door leads to the World Tree.

7. Step through the door and on the other side see the World Tree. The Word Tree is the largest tree you have ever seen. Its trunk extends out further than the eye can see going both left and right. The branches go up into the heavens and you cannot see the top of the tree. You can see that the roots go deep into the Earth.

8. This is the Center of the Otherworld, and it is your starting point. Until you are very proficient with traveling, you may want to start here.

9. Look above the mighty trunk and you will see the massive branches of World Tree. These branches go above into the clouds and deep into space and the cosmos. Look down and see the great roots of the world tree going down deep into the earth into the Underworld. You are at the center of the three worlds.

10. There are two ways I like to travel to the Otherworld, you can visualize a door in the trunk of the massive tree. State your intention on the part of the Otherworld you would like to go. Then simply open the door and walk through. The second way is when you are facing the World Tree, state your intention on where you would like to go and then around and face the opposite way. You are in the Otherworld already so you just need to turn around to the part of the Otherworld you wish to go.

11. When you arrive at the Otherworld, take note of the first thing you see? Explore the immediate environments carefully. When you are ready, go back the way you came and back to the trunk of the World Tree. Then state your intention to return back to your body.

12. After awakening from your journey, record your experience in your magickal journal and ground

yourself back to the physical plane. You may do this by eating something light, drinking water, and/or doing "everyday" things around your home.

Astral Exercise #3

1. Play your shamanic drumming recording if you have one as per the previous exercises.
2. Sit or lie in a comfortable position. Make sure your back is as straight as possible.
3. Close your eyes and take a few deep breaths.
4. Relax your body as best you can. Begin with your feet. Tell them to relax and release all tension. Then move up to your calf. Tell them to relax and release all tension. Go up to the thighs, glutes, back, belly, chest, shoulders, arms, hands, neck, and head in turn, telling them all to relax and release all stress and tension.
5. Visualize a spiral of light, beginning at your feet, spiraling around you, going clockwise; it surrounds your entire body. The only thing you are able to see is the spiral of light. Know that this magickal spiral of light is transporting you to the World Tree.
6. This is the Center of the Otherworld, your starting point. Until you are very proficient with traveling, you always want to start here.
7. Look above the mighty trunk and you will see the massive branches of World Tree. These branches go above into the clouds and deep into space and the cosmos. Look down and see the great roots of the world tree going down deep into the earth into the Underworld. You are at the center of the three worlds.
8. There are two ways I like to travel to the Otherworld, you can visualize a door in the trunk of the massive tree. State your intention on the part of the Otherworld you would like to go. Then simply open the door and walk through.

The second way is when you are facing the world tree, state your intention on where you would like to go and then around and face the opposite way. You are in the Otherworld already so you just need to turn around to the part of the Otherworld you wish to go.

9. When you arrive at the Otherworld, take note of the first thing you see? Explore the immediate environments carefully. When you are ready, go back the way you came to the trunk of the world tree. State your intention to return to your body.

10. After awakening from your journey, record your experience in your magickal journal and ground yourself back to the physical plane. You may do this by eating something light, drinking water, and/or doing "everyday" things around your home.

Your Otherworld Guide

It is very important to have a guide when you are journeying to the Otherworld. The Otherworld is a place both mysterious and beautiful, but can be very strange to the spirit traveler who is not accustomed to this world. There are many beings who can help you upon your path through this realm and many who delight in seeing you become lost and confused. Your Otherworld guide can help you find places of power, healing, and magick while keeping you away from the darker places that do not have your best interest at hand. Your Otherworld guide can also introduce you to Elves, Faeries, and help you find Otherworldly tools that will help you in works of healing and magick.

Finding your Otherworld Guide

1. Choose one of the astral exercises and travel to the World Tree.

2. Once there, make the following statement: "I wish to find my Otherworld Guide".

3. Look above the mighty trunk and you will see the massive branches of World Tree. These branches go above into the clouds and deep into space and the cosmos. Look down and see the great roots of the world tree going down deep into the earth into the Underworld. You are at the center of the three worlds.

4. There are two ways I like to travel to the Otherworld; you can visualize a door in the trunk of the massive tree. State your intention on the part of the Otherworld you would like to go. Then simply open the door and walk through. The second way is when you are facing the world tree, state your intention on where you would like to go and then around and face the opposite way. You are in the Otherworld already so you just need to turn around to the part of the Otherworld you wish to go.

5. Keep the intention to find your Otherworld Guide in your mind. Begin to explore the Otherworld. Trust your intuition. Look for people and animals along the way and ask them if they are your Otherworld Guide. If not, ask them to point out the direction in which you can find your guide.

6. Once you find a spirit who is a likely candidate to become your Otherworld Guide, ask if he or she is willing to help you navigate the Otherworld. If the answer is "no," the spirit is not your guide and you should keep looking. If the answer is "yes," ask for his or her name. Then ask your Guide if there is anything he or she would like in return. If the request is reasonable and you are able and willing to do it, then by all means do it. If not, graciously explain why you cannot meet the request.

7. Know that you can call upon your Guide each time you enter the Otherworld.

8. Come back to the World Tree the way you came. Then open your eyes and journal about your experiences.

Walking In Spirit

To walk in spirit is to literally walk in between the worlds. This is the magical practice of either opening a portal into the Otherworld while you are in the physical world or the ability to bring this world and the Otherworld together. There are many reasons why you may want to walk between the worlds. It is far easier to work with nature spirits and other entities of the Otherworld when we do this. It is also one of the best ways to see the astral counterpart to where we are in the physical world. You can see earth energies, ley lines, and spirit roads and the beings that travel upon them. You can also find hidden magical structures such as Faery mounds, spiral castles, and Elvish dwellings. In the Arthurian Grail Mysteries, Parzival is able to find the Grail Castle because he is walking in between the worlds. This is how we are able to sometimes stumble into the Otherworld. We go into a light trance when the veil between the worlds is thin and we are able to see Otherworldly things that seem to be in the physical plane. Raven Kaldera, in his book The *Pathwalker's Guide To The Nine Worlds,* calls this technique way-taming. Way-Taming, or *wonder,* is the English translation of one of Odin's titles, *Vegtamr.*

Going Forth To Walk In Spirit

1. Find a place in nature that you would like to take your spirit walk.
2. Take a few moments to center yourself and allow your thoughts to be of the Otherworld. Take a few deep breaths and connect with the energies of your natural space.
3. Visualize an energetic stream that is the concept of Time. See the past come to you at the present then wisp by you into the future.
4. Step outside of the time steam either physically or mentally or both. By stepping outside of the time stream, you are telling your consciousness that you are stepping

from the physical world and going into the Otherworld.

5. Now, take your finger or perhaps a magical wand or staff and cut a line into the air. You are cutting a magical doorway or curtain into the Otherworld. If you like you can use magical rune, symbol, or sigil instead. The choice is yours.

6. Walk through the magical entrance way into the Otherworld. Seal the entrance you made with your finger or wand. Re-trace the line with white light and see it seal behind you. You do not want anyone coming up behind you and accidentally going into the Otherworld.

7. Take your walk in spirit and explore the Otherworld. Take your time. What do you see? Are there entities or beings you can communicate with?

8. When you are ready, you can either go back the way you came or cut an entrance out of the Otherworld where you are.

9. Journal your experience.

Restoring Balance Between the Worlds

As witches and magical people, it is our responsibility to help in the process of restoring balance between our world and the Otherworld. There has been a lot of damage done to the relationships between humans and Otherworldly beings. It is going to be a great task to heal the rift that was created many years ago when humans no longer saw spirits of nature as a valued part of the land and greed took over. It will take many years, but it is up to us to continue the process of healing that was started by witches, pagans, and Spirit Walkers. We can start by rebuilding the trust that was lost. The first thing we need to do is begin working with Nature Spirits, Elves, and Faeries. These beings have a strong connection with the energetic cycles of nature. When we start cultivating relationships with the spirits of nature they will slowly begin to trust as. We also need to make sure we are healing our natural world in any way that we can. The spirits are watching to see how we treat nature and the land. We have to do than simply not cause more damage to the ecosystem. We need to be actively trying to heal the land. We can do this by both energy healing for the land as well as fight industries who are causing harm to our earth. Another thing we should be doing is working with the dragons of the land. Later on, in this book, we will learn about the regenerative earth power of dragons and how they affect the land and the earth as a whole. By working to understand these energies and building a relationship with these magnificent beings we will learn to have great power that we can use to heal the land. Once we learn to do these things the trust between us and Otherworld spirits will slowly start to be rebuilt and we can find balance between the worlds.

Chapter 3

Ecstatic Dance

The earth is made of energy that pulses and beats. When the Spirit Walker listens to this energy it seems to have a "rhythm" much like music. When the Spirit Walker listens closely to this music it begins to fill the body with the energies of healing and transformation. The body then begins to ride the musical energy like a wave transporting the Spirit Walker into another dimension of healing, sacredness, and transformation. Music is universal because energy is universal. The tempo and flow of music influences us because the rhythm and pacing harmonize with our mind causing a mild trance state. Our bodies, in turn, flow with the beat of music. Scientists say some energies come to us in waves. If you watch the waves and currents under the ocean, you see the energy moving underwater plant life. They seem to dance with the water currents. The beat of the Spirit Walker's drum or any other instrument echoes the pulse of the earth energies and fills our hearts with ecstatic dance. This dance causes us to embrace the earth energies in a rapture of movement and power.

To dance is to perform a sacred ceremony to the earth and all life upon it. Our bodies come from the earth so it is natural to celebrate the energies of the earth through movement and joy. No one has to tell us to dance. It is a part of our genetic makeup. It is a part of our heritage as children of the earth. When a baby hears music, they cannot help but to move with the sound. The child will do their best to synchronize themselves to the joy of dance.

Many tribal cultures have used dance as ritual and prayer to the earth and the spirits. The Native American tribes are one of many that use dance as ceremony and prayer. Every single

Native American tribe has their own special dances that celebrate rites of passage, the seasons and weather, sacred animals, war, peace, and many other things. Sadly, when the United States Government placed the Native Americans in reservations, they outlawed their spirituality which included any and all dances. Some of the people performed some of the dances in secret, such as the Lakota Sun Dance, and continue to be performed today. While, others have been all but forgotten. Fortunately, some observers documented several of the dances. In their book, *Indian Dances of North America,* Reginald and Gladys Laubin recount part of the Vision Dance that was held every year by the Delaware tribe:

> "Each visionary had a song concerning his vision. The leader now sang the words to a verse of his song and the singers used the song as a dance tune, striking the rolled hide in time. There were two fires in the Big House, one at each side of the center post. The leader danced counterclockwise in an oval around the two fires. He could stop the singers whenever he wanted by whooping. He might sing another verse, which the singers would sing after him as he danced again."

Another dance that seemed to be performed often was the eagle dance. There were many accounts of some type of eagle dance being performed by many different tribes. The eagle, of course, was considered the most sacred of all birds because it flew the highest. To the observations of the Native American people, Eagle flew very close to the Creator and, therefore, had special significance. I had been told once that Eagle flew so high towards Creator that Creator would often listen to the prayers of the people that Eagle would carry to him. The Cherokee people used the Eagle dance for a variety of purposes. It could be used for peace, war, healing, and many other things. The Lakota Sundance is still being performed even today. The Sundance is performed in the summer months for four days. There are people who drum and sing the sacred songs and other people who are there to support the dancers. The dancers dance for four days asking Creator for a vision, healing for themselves or others, or for a blessing for the community. With each dance, there is a connection to the Creator, the earth, the people, and Spirit that permeates through all things. With this act of prayer and devotion the Native people continue to listen to the song of Mother Earth and pray to her through dance.

There are many other spiritual traditions that honor the spirits through dance such as the African Diasporic religions such as Haitian Vodou and Cuban Yoruba. These cultures use dance to honor the spirits and the gods as well as to tell myths and stories in order to preserve their culture. The dances are also performed to share in community space and give offerings to the spirits. In her book *Dancing Wisdom: Embodied Knowledge in Haitian Vodou, Cuban Yoruba, and Bahian Candomble,* Yvonne Daniels says:

"Despite the incredible labor demands and resulting physical drain on the African-derived population during enslavement and post-emancipation period, dancing and music-making have offered some relief, potential rejuvenation, and the promise of ecstasy or transcendence. In the Americas, the dancing body allowed temporary escape from the extraordinary hardships of enslavement and continued as a primary vehicle of spiritual communication and for both spiritual and artistic expression."

Each of the dances have specific ritual meaning depending upon the spirit or god involved and the energies that are brought into the ceremony through the ritual dance. There are special colors, songs, chants, and musical sounds that are used to call upon each of the spirits. There are also certain body movements that are meant to bring about the energies of the gods and spirits as well. The music that is played is usually from drums and/or rattles. Ceremonial songs are sung as well. These things bring about the magical dance that is used to connect to the spiritual plane and commune with the spirits.

The dancers move their bodies by bending their knees and allowing their shoulders and hips to move as needed in order to call upon the spirit that the dance is dedicated to. They dance in a circle or spiral in order to connect to the astral and spiritual planes where the gods and spirits reside. Through the dancer's movement and gestures, the dancer uses their energy and life force to create a conduit or battery for the god or spirit to manifest in the physical plane. As they dance, the dancers merge the spiritual and astral planes with the physical plane. This causes a gateway for the spirit to "ride" the dancer. In other words, the dance becomes an invocation for the spirits.

It is considered a very high honor to be able to "horse" or become a vessel for the gods or spirits. For the time of the ceremony, the dancer IS that god or spirit. Their mannerisms and body language, through dance, will change to reflect the spirit that is being honored. Once a spirit had manifested with the dancer, they were asked to perform magick, divination, and healings. These sacred ceremonies are very important to the community because, not only does it bring much healing to them, but the dance is a way to pass along the lore and traditions of the African Diaspora as well as connect to their ancestors.

Ecstatic dance has been used since the beginning of the human race to heal and to journey into the three worlds. In South Africa, the Bushmen are known as the oldest living culture on Earth. These people reside in Namibia and the Kalahari. Scientists have shown that the Bushmen may have been the original people of the human race. Meaning, it is quite possible that all races originated from these people. The core of Bushman spiritual practice is ecstatic dance. These dances consist of the shaking and quaking the body in order to obtain a deep trance state.

When the trance is obtained through the dance, they are able to connect with the ancestors and god, healing, wisdom, and spiritual teachings.

To the Bushman, the Universe is filled with life force that they call n/om (pronounced similarly to mom). N/om connects us with the cosmic web and, therefore, the universe as a whole. Through this connection of lifeforce energy, they are able to connect to the ancestors, God, and animals. The dance is begun by everyone gathering around a fire. They then sing the sacred songs. The actual dance is begun when Bushmen stomps their feet, clap, and sing while circling the fire. Soon the n/om is built up in the body. This life force is like a wave energy that builds in and around the dancers. The songs are sung in order to continue to build upon the rising energy. The Bushman do not dance to the n/om energy, but rather, it is the energy that is riding them and making them move in such a way that becomes the trance dance. This energy is described at times like a powerful pure love of all things and of god. It is important for the dance that the music, energy, and song create an intense emotional love for all things.

The Bushman describe the ecstatic dance as akin to being cooked or boiled in a large pot. They say it is the life force and god heating your entire body in order to prepare you to journey into the three worlds and to heal the community as well as receive divine messages. When the n/om begins to rise, the body begins to shake and quake in a powerful way and the ancestors can be seen by the dancers. The ancestors have the power to help the dancers in their ceremony. Once the heat in the body is sufficiently hot, God drops a rope from the sky and attaches it to the belly. The belly begins to move and pump the energy throughout the dance. It is here when the Bushman can climb or journey into the heavens to speak with God. During the shaking of the dance, the dancer goes into a deep trance that allows them to go into the Otherworld and join with the creation process of the Universe.

The ecstatic dance is a powerful healing tool for the Bushman. When the dancer is hot and boiling with n/om they are engulfed in divine love for all things that is so overwhelming that they tremble and shake throughout the dance. In order to heal a member of the community, the dancer will hug the person and send them what they call a "nail". What they are actually sending sounds more like an intense ray of healing energy. The dancer also has the ability, through n/om to see illness and pull it out and, in its place, place healing energy back inside. The dance has the power to heal the community and the dancer as well. The Bushman believe that to continue to be a healer you must constantly keep your energies clean and the only way to do this is to continue to dance.

Ecstatic dance is seen in cultures other than pagan, as well. If we take a moment and look at the Whirling Dervishes, we will see a wonderful dance technique of bliss and the union with God. The Whirling Dervishes were established by Jalalu'ddin Rumi. Rumi was a Sufi teacher and mystic as well as a poet of Sufi teachings. Rumi was born on September 30, 1207 in Balk, Afghanistan. Because of both political and religion turmoil, his father moved his family to the city of Konya, Turkey. It was said that Rumi had memorized the Koran and had developed magical powers at a very young age. In 1210, Rumi studied for nine years with his teacher named Seyyid Burhan al-Din Muhaqqiq. They traveled extensively together and in that time, Rumi learned the teachings of the prophets. Upon the conclusion of nine years, Seyyid (a titled depicting lineage from the prophets), instructed Rumi to go out into the world and teach the holy teachings of the Sufi prophets and to heal those he came upon. By spending a great deal of time in prayer and meditation upon the presence of God, he was able to gain magical healing powers. It was said that his voice was so soothing he could heal people simply by the power of his voice and his teachings. He also had the power to see into one's past, present, and future.

Rumi spent many years teaching in great schools and had many students who loved him. In 1244, he came upon a fellow Sufi mystic named Shamsi Tabriz. Rumi and Shamsi instantly felt the strong presence of God within each other. They felt that they had each found a spiritual counterpart. Together, they exiled themselves with in a sanctuary for three months to experience the ecstasy and transcendence of God together as spiritual equals, yet, each learning from the other to go deeper into God's bliss. As the years went by, Rumi and Shams each taught the holy teachings of the Sufi prophets. They developed both their comradery and their spiritual knowledge of God. Rumi had no other spiritual equal than Shamsi. Rumi's students became increasingly jealous of Shamsi. They would often exile themselves together and when they were with the people, Rumi's attention was often focused on Shamsi. One night, Rumi's students found Shamsi in the gardens and stabbed him. As he died, Shamsi cried out to God and his physical body vanished.

Rumi spent months looking for his dear friend. He did not want to believe that Shamsi was dead. Finally, after many months of searching, he came to the realization that his friend was gone and he fell into a deep grief. Through his grief, Rumi went without food and drink and simply merged himself with the thought of God. It was then the spirits of heaven came to him and renewed his spirit. Through this magical transformation he knew Shamsi was energetically blending his essence with his. At last, Rumi was whole once more. After this transformation, Rumi invented the dance of the Whirling Dervishes. In the book *The Whirling Dervishes,* Shems Friedlander says:

"One day, he was walking by the goldbeater's shop, he heard the hammers of the apprentices pounding the rough sheets of gold into beautiful objects. With each step he repeated the name of God; and now with the sound of hammers beating the gold, all he heard was 'Allah, Allah'. 'Allah, Allah' became every sound he heard and he began to whirl in ecstacy in the middle of the street. He unfolded his arms like a fledgling bird, tilted his head back, and whirled, whirled, whirled to the sound of 'Allah' that came forth from the very wind he created by his movement."

The Whirling dance is called the Sema and is performed in order for the dervish to transcend the limitations of the physical world and "fly" up to the heavens for the union of God. They dress in a tall conical hat that represents the tomb stone. His white flowing skirt represents the shroud and the black cloak represents the tomb or grave itself. To begin with the dervishes will say the holy prayers. Then the dervishes enter the dance area. The head dervish, called the *sheikh* leads them around in a circle three time. Then he stands with his head bowed as the dervishes each approach him and kiss his hand. Once they do this, they remove their cloaks. This represents being released from the tomb upon death to soar up to heaven to be with God. Once the cloak is removed, he crosses his arms upon his chest and begins to whirl counter clockwise at a moderate pace. Then the dervish gracefully unfolds his arms and lifts them up. This is when the dervish embraces God. The right arm and palm face the sky in order to receive the celestial energies of God. The left arm and palm are faced down in order to give the celestial energies back to the earth. As you can see, the dervish becomes a spiritual conduit for divine energy. During the entirety of the dance, the dervish repeats the name of God and become lost in the love and grace of God.

The witch's dance has been both fantasized about and feared for hundreds of years. Witches were said to dance around the devil in order to give him worship and receive his favors of black magick. This observation is a bastardization of a sacred dance in

Traditional Witchcraft that we call "Treading the Mill'". I can only imagine the poor Christian who stumbled upon the secret ritual of the old-time witches circling around The Magister or Horned figure. I can just see the fear in the eyes as they saw these witches chanting and raising power to weave their magick during the full moon. Treading the Mill is a dance that we use to raise power and bring ourselves into a state of trance so that we may work magick, cast spells, and honor the spirits of land, sky, and the ancestors.

Like most magical practices in Trad Craft, the dance is very simple but has a very powerful effect. To begin with, all the participants gather around the circle. In the middle of the circle is either a small fire or the coven candle placed in a lantern. The witches will then begin to walk around the circle in a counterclockwise or widdershins motion. One of the reasons for the widdershins motion is because we are guiding the energies in an anti-sunwise motion. The energies are going away from the normal everyday routine of our daily lives. We are going beyond Fate and circumstance to weave our magick in the way that our Divine Will and our spirits desire. Another reason for the widdershins motion is to tell our conscious minds that we are turning off our everyday mental chatter and moving towards our subconscious minds in order to move deeper into the magick of our own being. Some covens chant or beat a drum, but this is not necessary to work an effective mill dance. After a while, everyone will begin to walk faster and faster until the walk turns into a trot or gallop. You feel like you are running but it is more of a trot than anything else. Once the ritual leader feels the energies are at their peak, we will all grab hands, take a deep breath and send the energy around to each member then up and over the circle. It is then we do our magick.

Treading the Mill is more complex and powerful than it seems. When we first begin walking around the circle, we focus our minds and our breaths for the magick at hand. We know we are performing a very old and magical act and it is very profound. Some may gaze upon the fire in the center of the circle in order to maintain their equilibrium during the dance. As we circle around, we take deep breaths bringing in the magick of land, stars, and sky around us. Our minds begin to shift and go into a light trance. Once we begin walking faster and faster our attention closes in into the circle and its energies. This blocks out the world beyond the circle and focuses both our minds and magick on the work at and. For me, it feels like we are trotting our way between the worlds and weaving our magical Will like a powerful thread into the tapestry of Fate.

There are many things that can be done with the magick of Treading the Mill. The first thing I learned to do with the energies is to scry into the dark spaces in between each witch in the circle to see the past, present, and future. I would see the fate lines as they were coming near the coven and all that we had to do in the coming months or years. Another thing that happens with the Mill is that even those who are not advanced in their clairvoyant skills are able to see the Witch Ancestors, Elves, and other spirits who stand at the perimeter of the circle. Also, the magick of the Mill dance is that the witches in the circle can take the raised power and direct it towards our magical goal; be it to work our Will or to use it for healing.

When you tread the mill with sacred magical intention, you align yourself to all witches who have ever been, all witches who are, and all witches who ever will be. This dance brings you in between time and space and aligns you with the powers of the land, ancestors, and the universe. Treading the Mill is one of my favorite dances that brings me into trance. Because it is so simple it can be taught to anyone who is willing to put their waking consciousness aside to work magick and attune themselves to the witches of long ago and align ourselves to the powers of the old gods.

Ecstatic Dance

The Universe is movement and vibration. Everything from light and gamma rays of deep space to the stones upon the earth vibrate. Of course, light vibrates much faster than stone. But yet, stone still vibrates but at a much slower rate. Every atom moves. Movement in the Universe is constant. The galaxies are moving faster and faster away from the initial point of the big bang and the earth revolves around the sun. Here on Earth, water moves with the wind and the tides of the moon while plants grow through the earth to reach the light. Movement is our eternal constant force. When movement stops the process of atrophy and decay sets in. In our physical bodies when we do not move and exercise our bones lose density, our muscles atrophy, and we are more prone to disease. We must move our bodies to remain healthy and connected to the earth and the Universe.

As we have seen above, dance can be found in many different cultures around the world. Originally, it is thought that dance was a spiritual or religious expression. We can see that many different cultures use dance to connect with the energies of the gods, ancestors, and nature. Dance is a prayer that is in motion. Not only are we directing energy with our thoughts, emotions, and energies, but we are directing energies with our entire bodies. We are using our entire being to commune with spirits, heal, and bend energies to our Will. In order for us to work magick through dance we must go into a trance and connect with the life force around us. We must connect to the powers of the earth and allow the vibrations to overcome our senses and take us into the Otherworld.

Once you understand the mechanics on how ecstatic dance works, it is one of the easiest trances and magical techniques you will find. There are few things to keep in mind when you are performing an ecstatic dance. The first thing is to not worry about how you look to others. The Bushman never worry about how they look to outsiders, nor do most tribal people. If you have the opportunity to attend a drum jam or other earth based religious dance you will see that the movements are very individual and they are so attuned to spirit that they only care of the ecstasy they are feeling and not how they appear to others. Another thing to keep in mind is to allow the energies, or life force, to build up inside you and feel a great love for spirit, the earth, and the Universe. Then, allow the energies to take over your body and begin to move. Allow your entire body to move as it will, or more correctly, how the energies will. As with all magick, you must believe that you will be able to work magick with dance. I teach all my students, especially beginners, that when you are not sure what is going on or even if the magick is going to work that for right now just suspend disbelief. Our minds are powerful and will manifest what we believe or will block what we do not believe. The last thing to remember is that ecstatic dancing is very visceral and tactile. You may feel the energies and the Otherworld more than you see it. In essence, to feel the spirit and have a connection through your heart is just as valid as seeing them with clairvoyant site. Ideally, you will be able to do both, but to begin with, feeling the energy is a very good start.

The part of the dance that creates an ecstatic dance is emotion. When we combine strong emotions with trance dance it becomes ecstatic. The kind of emotions I am talking about is spiritual ecstasy, love, joy, and excitement. Yasmin Henkesh in her book *Trance Dancing With The Jinn: The Ancient Art of Contacting Spirits Through Ecstatic Dance* describes the difference between trance and ecstasy:

"Those who practice mysticism often understand ecstasy as the experience of the divine or union with the Creator. Ultimately, both terms describe altered states, but ecstasy involves heightened emotions, whereas trance may be induced by calming emotions (meditation). Nevertheless, both conditions share a common trait-narrow focused attention."

In order to bring emotions that bring about ecstatic dance it may help to do some emotional recall. Emotional recall is when you remember an experience that brought about the emotions that you wish to experience. For instance, if I wanted to conjure forth the emotion of spiritual connection or ecstacy, I would remember times in my life that I was overwhelmed by the joys and love of spirit. Like when I was ordained as a minister or when I drove to the top of a mountain for the first time after I made my chanupa (sacred pipe). I would recall these emotions and let them take over my energies and my body. So, for you, think of a few different times you felt spiritual ecstasy. Was it at a ritual or ceremony? Where you feeling a connection to mother earth while in a natural landscape? Was it witnessing a birth? Or perhaps as you gaze upon the stars at night? As you dance remember these spiritual events and bring to your heart these emotions. As you hold on to this feeling of ecstacy and connection let the memories of the events fade away and continue to dance.

Breathing Trance Techniques

We go into a trance all the time. When we are daydreaming, we are in trance. When someone is talking to us and we drift off for a moment, that is a trance. Also so is getting lost in a good song and becoming caught up in your thoughts when you jog or exercise. I remember when I was first learning magick I thought that a "true" trance is when you are so deep into a trance that people can call your name and you would never hear them. This is so far from the truth. In truth, in order to do effective magick with trance, especially ecstatic dance, you must be able to go into a trance while you dance and at the same time visualize energies and the spirits and work your Will. Being so deep into trance that you are lost is not an effective way to do magick. A very simple, yet effective way to induce trance is with specialized breathing techniques. I have been using breathe techniques to put myself into trance for many years. These techniques are very effective a one of my all-time favorites.

Sob Breathing

Sob breathing is pretty much how it sounds. You are going to breath as if you are sobbing. To do this, take three quick short inhalations through the mouth and one long exhalation. Like this: in, in,in, oooooouuuuuuut. Repeat as many times as you need to go into a trance.

Short Quick Breathing

This is essentially controlled hyperventilation. In order to do this technique, you take many short and quick in and out breaths through the mouth. Like this: In, out, in, out, in, out, in, out. It sounds like a dog panting but even quicker. Be mindful not to actually hyperventilate when performing this exercise.

Long Deep Breaths

This technique is exactly how it sounds. You are simply taking long deep breaths in and long deep breaths out. Iiiiiiiiiiiiiiiiinnnn, oooooouuuuuuttttttt, iiiiiiiiiiiiiiinnnn, oooooooouuuuuut. I like this technique a lot because it slows down my mind a great deal and allows me time to breath in energies as well.

Chaotic Breathing

This one is my absolute favorite. It is powerful, quick, and effective. You are combining all the above techniques. Sob breathing, short quick breaths, and long deep breaths. Do this over and over until you reach a trance. When performing this technique do not edit or judge what is happening. Just remember all three breathing techniques and perform them as you will. You can do them in order or out of order. I prefer to jumble them all up. I feel I get into a better trance that way.

Exercise: Trance Dance

1. Find music that makes you feel invigorated and spiritual. You can use drumming music, electronic dance music, or pagan chants.
2. Feel free to light incense of your choice. This is not a must, but it may help you in the beginning.
3. Plant your feet firmly on the ground and allow your upper body and arms to remain loose.
4. Take a deep breath of the earth energy around you. There is earth energy in the air, the sky, the waters, and the earth itself. Breath this into your belly.
5. Listen to the music and begin to move your hips. Remember not to edit yourself. Move freely as the music and energies take you.
6. Continue to breath and allow the earth energies to build up in your body.
7. Move your feet, your hips, and your chest. Allow your arms and hands to move as they will according to the movement of the earth energies in your body. You can also add a bounce to your dance if you like.
8. Begin to add the breathing trance techniques. Sob breathing, short quick breathing, deep breathing, and chaotic breathing.
9. As you ride the waves of energies with the music and dance, focus on your heart and begin feeling the spirits, gods, and ancestors. Send them energy through your heart and, in turn, allow them to send you energy.
10. Bring yourself to a place of spiritual bliss. You may use spiritual recall by remembering time in your life you felt the bliss of spirit. Continue dancing and going into trance through breath.
11. Open your eyes, if closed, and try to see the spirits. You

may see shadows, fog, wavy lines, or you may see the spirits clearly. You may also see the spirits in your mind's eye or just have a "knowing" they are there. These are all signs you are starting to see spirits. Keep practicing they will appear more clearly as you become proficient with the technique.

12. When you are ready to give thanks to the spirits who joined in your dance and ground the remaining energy. You may give the energy to the earth as a sacred offering.

Chapter 4

Seidr-Sorcery of the Otherworld

"Odin had the skill, that brings the greatest power, and worked it himself. It is called seidr, and by means of it he could know the fate of men and foretell events that had not yet come to pass. He could work the death of men or loss of luck or sickness. So also could he take the wits and strength from some people and give to others." -*Ynglingasaga*

In the Nordic and Heathen spirituality there is a magical practice that is called *seidr*. I have heard the term pronounced a few different ways. It can be pronounced "say-th", "seeth", or "sigh-th". Seidr was described in the Northern European sagas and other works from 900-1100 CE, most notably by Snorri Sturluson. These stories describe both women and men who work magick to speak with the dead for prophecy, cause storms, bend the will of noblemen, shapeshift and many other things. In these stories, there is little that is described about the magical techniques except for a few excerpts that exist in the sagas and even then, you have to piece them all together to even begin to get a clear picture of the magick that was performed. Edred Thorsson in his book *Witchdom Of The True: A Study of the Vana-Troth and the Roots of Seidr* says:

"It is most likely that the noun has been derived from the strong verb *sida* "to work sorcery", the simple past tense of which *seid*, 'I performed sorcery'. There is also a phrase: *seida seid* 'To work sorcery'. The Vibrant and rich history of the word makes it appear that the world is fairly old in the language, and that it has not been recently borrowed from a neighboring language."

As we know in modern witchcraft and magical practice there are different skills in magick. We have the "active" magical power that sends out spells, healing, and conjurations of the spirits. There is also the "receptive" magical power that involve trance states, scrying, seeing spirits, and spirit communication. Both of these "powers" are necessary for the adept magical practitioner, but they are different talents. Some people are naturally more proficient in one more than the other, but I feel it is of great importance to be skilled in both. For myself, I am a naturally strong sender. When I first learned how to cast spells and send out energy, I could really throw out some magick. But I was determined to learn to see spirits and scry with the best of magicians. I practiced every day until I was blue in the face. During my practice, I quickly learned that trance techniques came easy to me. In Seidr, there are also two different magical skill sets of active and receptive magick. There is the active magical technique of shaking and swaying that puts the practitioner into a trance in order to work a variety of types of magick. Then, there is the receptive magical technique of going into a trance to journey into the Otherworld for the purpose of prophecy. We call this Oracular Seidr in our modern practice.

The Web of Wyrd

The Web of Wyrd is another term for the Cosmic Web, which means that all things are connected energetically and spiritually and yet it is more complicated than this simple explanation. The Nordic people have a very interesting idea of what *wyrd* is. In our modern English language, the closest that we can come up with to define this term is that it is loosely a combination of Fate, Destiny, and Karma, and yet is not these things. Take a moment and imagine a large spider web with its crisscrossing threads. Now expand on that thought and imagine that the spider's web is now three dimensional. These multilayered threads connect us to the earth, plants, animals, humans and the stars. They even connect us to the past, present, and future. The energies of wyrd say that all of your actions, thoughts, and deeds affect your present day and your future. In quantum physics, there is a theory that states that not only do events from the past flow forward to effect the present, but at the same time, events from the future flow backward to affect the present as well. Meaning, both past and future are affecting us right here and now. There are many other things in the Universe that effect these energies. One of the most important things to affect your wyrd is your family karma. Yes, the actions and deeds of your forebears have a direct outcome of your present energies. I, personally, do not believe in the concept of "the sins of the father" but there is something called "family karma". With family karma, the actions of your ancestors energetically effect the bloodline of your family both physically and spiritually. This is one of the reasons why some pathologies are passed down from one generation to another. It is also the reason why families tend to stay locked in their economic situation. Energetically, what happens with family karma is that when there is great trauma, be it physically, emotionally, or spiritually, it sends a reverberation down the energetic bloodlines that connect your ancestors to you. There are many ways to remedy family karma but we do not have the time here in this book. I give explicit details how to heal family karma in my book *Deeper Into The Underworld: Death, Ancestors, and Magical Rites.*

People that you come in contact with throughout your life affects your wyrd as well. When you fall in love, learn life lessons, and make choices with family, lovers, and friends this all has an impression on your wyrd. We are constantly learning and growing with these life lessons so, too, is your wyrd changing and altering. When we establish a relationship with someone, both positive and negative, both parties influence each other's wyrd. The purpose of this is to spiritually evolve and grow. When we have learned the lessons with our relationships, they either grow into a deeper healthier relationship or the relationship ends. When a relationship ends it is not good or bad. It means that the wyrd between the two of you has obtained all the spiritual growth it can do and it is time to sever the relationship to make room for another relationship.

How we treat the earth, plants, and animals also has an effect on our wyrd. As we know, the earth is sacred and holy and how we treat our Mother impacts our wyrd. Likewise, the animals, plants, stones, and all of the inhabitants of the earth should be treated like our brothers and sisters. In the 21st Century, more and more people are getting cancer along with a plethora of other pathologies. If we take a moment to observe our earth and our surroundings, we will see that our earth has been polluted with toxic chemicals. Not only is the climate changing with these things, but so is our bodies and our health. We are all connected by wyrd.

Our wyrd is woven by the Three Norns. Their names are Urdr (That which became), Verdandi (That which is becoming now), and Skuld (That which should come to pass). These three sisters weave the web of wyrd into the great cosmic tapestry. This great tapestry is woven deep in the Underworld at the Well of Urdr. Not even the gods are immune from wyrd. The Norns' web flows through the nine worlds encompassing the wyrd of human, god, giant, elf, and the dead. None can escape it. It has been said that only the Norns can influence or change the web of wyrd. But what of witches and magicians? Are we not magical? Do we not influence what is coming and what should come to pass? As magical practitioners, we have the power to influence the Universe with our magick. We can change the outcome of the future with spells and sorcery. This is the purpose of the magick of seidr. Granted, anything that the Norns have Fated to come to pass no amount of magick can change. Like they say in the television show, *Doctor Who,* "It's a fixed point in time."

Sorcery of Seidr: Shaking and Swaying

Shaking and swaying seidr is magical movement. It puts us in a mystical trance and allows us to change ourselves and the world around us. It is a dance, but not quite a dance. It is trance, but not quite a trance. It is a practice of movement that is "in between" and allows us to go in between the worlds in order for us to weave our own strands on the Web of Wyrd.

The shaking and swaying trance technique was popularized by Jan Fries in his book *Seidways: Shaking, Swaying and Serpent Mysteries.* In his groundbreaking book, he discusses his theory of how the seidrmen and women must have shaken and swayed themselves into a deep trance so that they may perform great feats of magick. In his research, he found this technique was akin to "seething" the quaking and shaking of the body. Modern Nordic authors disagree whether the term *seidr* could be where we get the term "seeth" from. The Sagas and the Eddas do not specify what magical techniques were used for seidr sorcery but we can hypothesize that they may have been influenced by other shamanic techniques from Finland and perhaps Russia. Even if the shaking and swaying seidr technique is not exactly what was practiced it is a very powerful and useful magical technique indeed.

The Sagas and Eddas describe many instances that seidr was used for sorcery and magick. There are stories that tell us how the sorcerers would bring up terrible storms and send them to their enemies. The seidrmen and women could protect warriors from being cut by the sword's blade. One story relates how a seidrwoman enchanted her lover so that he could find no peace in Iceland until he returned to her. There are also stories about how seidr workers would hire themselves out to perform magick for their clients. Seidr workers did many works of magick. They performed magical acts such as healings, divination, protection, love spells, shapeshifting, and justice magick. The Sagas and Eddas only give us a fraction of what was the legacy of the sorcery of seidr.

To shake and sway or to "seeth" is similar to ecstatic dance. They both use erratic movement, breath, and earth energies to bring you into a trance state. There are a few differences that I want to go over before we get started with the technique. To seidr, you must be warmed up, even more so than for ecstatic dance. Sometimes seidr movements can get very "jerky" and can have some wild and chaotic moves. You may want to stretch beforehand. If you cannot stretch before hand for whatever reason then you MUST start the seidr slowly and work your way up to faster movements. I have pulled muscles and given myself headache by not preparing properly. The other difference is that there are no dance steps per se and no rhythm to it. Granted, if seething to a drum beat you may move your body with the sound of the drum but this is not the goal. The goal is to let your mind and your inhibitions go and allow your body to chaotically move. The chaotic moving of the body in seidr tends to confuse the rational mind and allows a deeper trance to set in. When this happens, your mind has the freedom to trance out, journey, and do magical workings.

Shaking and Swaying Seidr Technique

I prefer to do seidr outdoors in nature but you can perform it indoors as well. If you are working indoors be mindful that the shaking and swaying can cause the floors to creak and make noise. If you live with others this may be a nuisance. Feel free to light incense, light your candles, and have someone drum for you (or play pre-recorded drumming music). Personally, I do not use drumming when I perform seidr. I tune in to the earth energy around me and allow those energies and my breath to be my drum beat. You do not have to do what I do. Feel free to experiment as you like.

1. Place your feet shoulder width apart and bend your

knees slightly. Begin taking deep breaths. You may use one of the breathing trance techniques if you like.

2. Begin swaying left to right and back again. Keep taking deep breaths. This is the only step that is similar to a dance. You will simply sway by placing your body weight on your left foot then right foot (or vice versa).

3. Next, begin to slightly bounce. The bounce is coming from your lower legs, but allow it to shake your entire body. Keep bouncing as you do this.

4. Continue with your trance inducing breath then begin swaying your hips back and forth. You can make circles with your hips if you prefer. Whichever feels more natural to you.

5. Now, start bouncing a little harder at a moderate pace. Take a moment to feel this in your entire body.

6. At this point, move your shoulders and chest in whatever way feels natural to you. You can allow your arms, chest, and shoulders to jerk back and forth. Keep your arms and shoulders loose while you do this. This may feel odd at first so take a moment to get used to this feeling.

7. This is where the fun begins. Keeping all these steps in mind (swaying, bouncing, moving hips, chest, and shoulders) move faster and in any direction you like. This is chaotic moving. Move all over the place. Do not plan the movement of the body. Just move. All over the place. In all directions.

8. Allow your head to slightly be loose. Be mindful not to hurt your neck. You can raise your shoulders to support the back of your head as it hangs loose.

9. Keep breathing. Allow your mind to let go. If it helps, think of it as your consciousness is following the chaotic movement of your body. Allow the trance to naturally occur. This may take a few practice sessions for you to feel comfortable enough to let your mind go completely.

10. What did you see in your trance? What perceptions did you have? What intuitions did you feel?

Seeing Fate on the Strands of Wyrd

As we have discussed in this chapter, the Web of Wyrd connects all things with an invisible energetic thread or web. Remember, all things are connected. The closer that things are in relationship then the closer the thread. Anyone you have a relationship with your strands of weird will be very close together. Likewise, people you never met and will likely never meet, your strands may not cross at all. However, they are still connected. This is one of the reasons that we are able to do magick for and on people as well as do divinations for them. Even if we have no direct relationship with someone or something, you can trace the energetic strands of weird and eventually find the connections with that person or thing.

As magical people, we have the ability to see the "Fate" of people. Fate is rather a misnomer. When we see someone's fate, we are not seeing the fixed unchangeable event in someone's life. We are seeing the events that are down someone's path if circumstances as they are now stay exactly the same. Fate is changeable. The whole point of doing a reading or divination for someone is to either prevent things from happening or to encourage good things to continue to come their way. With the shaking and swaying seidr technique you can look down someone's Web of Wyrd for divination. Essentially, what you are doing is scrying down someone's Wyrd or Fate strand. When we visualize someone's Wyrd strand, it is not the tiny thing spider web strand, but instead a large strand that is easy to see the images for what is to come.

Shaking and Swaying Seidr Magick (Visioning)

1. Perform the shaking and swaying technique from the previous exercise.

2. Allow your consciousness to go into a trance.

3. Visualize the person, animal, thing, or situation you are divining for in front of you. You can also close your eyes and see the object of your focus in your mind.

4. See how their Wyrd strand is connected to you and to the Universe. At this point, you may see the strand and how it is connected to everything else or you may see it as a long strand that goes out into the Universe or the beyond.

5. Visualize the Wyrd strand expanding and becoming just as large as the person, animal, or thing in question. How you perceive the strand is up to you, but I see it as a large energetic tunnel. Sometimes I see it as red, sometimes as white, or blue. The color is not important but is important that you visualize the large strand as clearly as you can.

6. As you seidr, focus your attention on the images coming down the Wyrd strand. These are the images that are coming to pass. I tend to see the images coming towards me from within the tunnel. When you see an image of interest, you can mentally ask the image to stop moving and to show you more. The image may then play out like a movie and show you in greater detail what is to pass. You may also use this technique to see the past. Simply reverse the flow of the images in your mind and see what images are going away from the person to the tunnel. These events are being woven into the fabric of the Web of Wyrd.

7. When you have seen all you wish to see bring your seidr to a close.

Performing Seidr Magick

We learned in this chapter that the seidrmen and women used their seidr magick for sorcery. They used this powerful technique to change the weather, bring healing, protection, love, and to curse. Now we will use the shaking and swaying seidr technique to cause change in the Universe in accordance with our Will and our energies. When we learn basic magick and spellcasting techniques we are taught to go into a light trance and build up the magical energy while maintaining our focus on our desired outcome. We are taught that to build up the sufficient magical power we must chant, drum, or dance. With the shaking and swaying seidr technique we are taking the "build up of power" to the next step. We are connecting to the Web of Wyrd to work our will with the magick of seidr. In her book *Nine Worlds of Seid-Magic: Ecstasy and Neo-Shamanism In North European Paganism,* Jenny Blain says:

"So for at least some within today's Heathen community, seidr, defined as use of hidden skills which enable the practitioner to contact spirits and with their aid to 'see along' the threads of orlog or Wyrd or actively manipulate those threads, is legitimate and acceptable practice when performed for the benefit of the community."

Shaking and Swaying Seidr Magick (Sorcery)
1. Perform the shaking and swaying technique from the previous exercise.
2. Allow your consciousness to go into a trance.
3. Connect with the energies of the land around you. Connect with the magick of the landscape that you are in. Connect with the energies of the stars, the air, the planets, and all things.
4. As you are shaking and swaying, breath in the fires of the earth into your body. Feel the power of the earth build up in your body and your aura around you.
5. At this time, visualize your goal. See the outcome of your goal as clearly as you can. Continue to breath and begin shaking and swaying with more power.

6. As you build up the power of the earth with the shaking and swaying seidr techniques, see your goal more clearly and clearly with each shake.

7. Now, visualize the outcome manifesting in front of you and around you. See yourself in the middle of your goal. If it is writing a book, see yourself holding the book. If it is a new job, see yourself performing the job. If you are doing a healing see the person healed and happy.

8. When you feel the power is built up to the maximum that it could possibly be, see your target (outcome) in front of you and take a deep breath. On the exhale, send all the energy you have built up to the target. See the target absorb all of the magick.

9. Know that you have influenced the Web of Wyrd with your magick.

10. Bring your seidr session to an end and ground any excess energy you may have.

Shaking and Swaying Seidr Ritual

I often use the seidr techniques alone and outside of ritual. If you feel called to do this type of magick in a ritual context I think that could be very powerful indeed. If you would like to turn the seidr techniques into a ritual you can follow this simple outline:

1. Clear the area of any debris so that you will not stumble. If outdoors never banish. Everything that is there, lives there. You would not want someone banishing you out of your home.

2. Say aloud your magical intention. This tells the spirits what is happening and they can choose to help your magick if they Will.

3. Call upon your god and goddess to aide in the magick of your rite. If you like, you can also call upon Odin and Freya to guide and empower your magick.

4. Call upon your ancestors to aid in the magick and also to protect your rite from energetic and physical intruders.

5. Perform one of the seidr techniques. You may simply commune with the spirits, perform divination, or you may perform sorcery.

6. Once your magical portion is complete, give offerings of wine or mead to the gods, land spirits, and the Ancestors.

7. Give thanks to the gods, land spirits, and the Ancestors. Use your own words that come from your heart. I have found the best way to thank the spirits is not form some written script but to give genuine thanks from your heart.

8. The rite has ended.

Oracular Seidr

Oracular Seidr is the term we use in our modern times to describe the magical rite of traveling in spirit to the Otherworld in order to speak with the spirits for prophecy. The Sagas and the Eddas have many tales in which the seer, who can be either a man or woman, prophecies what is to pass. It was a common practice for seers and sorcerers to travel the country side to practice their magick for noblemen and women for a fee. Magical people would often charge for their craft. Just as in our modern times, they needed to pay for shelter, food, and clothing like anyone else. The seidrmen and women of antiquity were not taking advantage of their rich clients, but were charging what they felt was a fair price for the service they provided. When a person practicing seidr came to your dwelling it was a huge affair. The seidr practitioner was treated very well. They were the guest of honor and given gifts, money, and a great feast. The most complete tale of this come from the Saga of Eric The Red.

One winter in Greenland there was a famine. Many people were starving because there was little food and very little game that was caught by the hunters. The people had heard of a great seidrwoman named Thorbyorg. Thorkell was the farmer who held the most land and it was up to him to send for Thorbyorg so that she may use her magick to foretell the future for the people. When she arrived, she was dressed in a beautiful blue cloak and held a magical staff that was inlaid with jewels and precious stones. Thorkell was excited to see her, but even more excited to hear her prophecies. He asked her to tell his people the future, but it was not the time. Thorbyorg insisted she spend the night in his home, but first she was to have a magnificent magical feast. Her feast consisted of the heart from one of every barnyard animal on the farmstead. The next day, she sat on the high seat which was prepared for her. She asked for the sacred songs of seidr to be sung for her but no one remembered the songs except one woman. The woman sang so beautifully that she enchanted everyone with delight. Thorbyorg went into a deep trance and journeyed to the Otherworld. She told the people that the famine was soon to pass and spring would come soon to relieve their troubles. She allowed everyone to come up to her and ask her a question. She gave her answers and everything she spoke of came to pass.

There is some lively conversation in the seidr and Heathen communities about whether seidr is a form of shamanism. We are not exactly sure where the word "shaman" comes from but archeologists believe it comes from either the Manchu-Tungus or the Evenki word "saman". The shamans of Siberia used spirit journeying, soul retrieval, and heal the sick from spirit intrusions in their healing practices. They travel in spirit up and down a world tree with branches stretching up into the Upperworld and roots that went deep into the Underworld. We can see some similarities with the cosmology of the Siberian shamans and the Nordic Heathens. As we have learned, in Heathen cosmologies, the gods and spirits travel up and down the world tree called Yggdrasil. Both shamanism and oracular seidr use drums in their ceremonies and both spirit travel upon a world tree.

Modern Oracular Seidr was first started by the Heathen

author Diana Paxson. She tells us that she attended classes on core-shamanism by Michael Horner. She was inspired by his shamanic techniques of journeying to the three worlds in order to find wisdom, meet spirit contacts and heal the sick. There are only very few literary tales of oracular seidr. The tale of *Eric The Red* is the only resource that we have that goes into detail about the seeress and the ceremony that she performed for her prophecies. The other stories in the Sagas and Eddas only briefly speak of seeresses who are able to tell the future. It was customary for large landowners to host the seidr men and women and prepare a large feast for them so that they may predict the future. In *Arrow-Odd's Saga,* translated by Stephen E. Flowers and James A. Chisholm, they tell the tale of a seeress named Heid, "She traveled widely to feasts, to which farmers invited her, throughout the land. She told people their fates and forecasting the weather for the coming winter and other things."

We know that Modern Oracular Seidr was influenced by modern day core-shamanism. There are a few differences between the two practices. Oracular Seidr, the way I was taught, focuses on obtaining prophecies and oracles from the dead in the ancestral realm of Helheim. They do not necessarily travel the worlds in order to heal the sick, but they can gather information from the spirits about how to treat the ailing person. One of the core practices in shamanism is that the shaman will have many spirit contacts. They do not really do this in Oracular Seidr. In my research and experience with Oracular Seidr, they also do not remove spirit institutions as they do in traditional shamanic practice. It is safe to say, that there are many core-shamanic influences in oracular seidr, but they are not necessarily the same. They are two different cultures with different techniques and different ways to approach the three worlds and the spirits. In my opinion, it is not important how close Oracular Seidr is with shamanism because seidr is a magical technique that has an interesting and powerful history all on its own. There is no need to try to validate it by comparing it to shamanism.

Protection of the Ancestors

Every day, before I go to bed a take a candle from my god and goddess altar and energetically bless my home by drawing the rune Algiz and Othala. Algiz means protection and Othala means ancestral land or the home where the ancestors are. As I ask for the blessings of the gods, I see my ancestors energetically form a protective circle around my home. This is one of the most powerful protective techniques that I use. I did not come up with this on my own. After years of working with my ancestors it just happened one day all on its own. The ancestors protect me and my living space.

When you perform oracular seidr, it is a good practice to ask our ancestors to protect you from negative energies or spirits. In my book *Deeper Into The Underworld: Death, Ancestors, and Magical Rites* I teach how the ancestors protect your ancestor altar and your magical space form negative energies. This is essentially the same technique. In order to do this, I call to my ancestral line with my heart. Remember, the heart chakra and the heart itself, is the energetic home of the ancestors. Your heart pumps your blood and the blood carries the DNA of your entire family line. To connect with the ancestors, you must reach out to them with your heart. See them in your heart chakra. Have the longing and desire for your ancestors to appear and protect your magical space or home. Then visualize them encircling your magical working space.

Modern Oracular Seidr

"One point that many seidr practitioners make is that learning to do seidr is taught through doing it, and that the 'teachers' are not so much other practitioners as those met within the journey: which again fits with traditional shamanic, and present-day no-shamanic accounts. Teachers may be ancestors, animal 'allies', spirit of the land or of plants, the Norns, deities including Odinn himself." Jenny Blain, *"Nine Worlds of Seid-Magic: Ecstasy and neo-shamanism in North European Paganism"*.

In our modern times, many seidr workers have taken Diana Paxson's oracular seidr right, called the High Seat Rite, and made it their own. I would like to take a moment and go over a few of the common elements that are found in High Seat Rite. The rite is done for a group but can be adapted for the solitary practitioner. The seer sits on a special seat that is slightly elevated from the attendees. He or She wears a cloak and carries a staff. These tools are to help the seer go into trance and travel to the Otherworld. Then there are drummers and singers who help build up the energy of the rite as well as bring the seer and the attendees into trance. Sometimes, there is a circle of protection that is cast around the ritual space. Once the drummers and singers build up the energy, there is a guided visualization that helps bring the entire congregation into the Underworld. At the Pagan Spirit Gathering in 2007, I had the privilege of attending Diana Paxson's High Seat Rite. She took us down to Helheim (Nordic Realm of the Dead) through a guided meditation. It was the coolest experience to travel down into the Underworld as a large group. Then, the attendees are instructed to stay outside the gates of Helheim as the seer go into the gates and calls upon the ancestors. One by one, the attendees are allowed the ask the seer questions. The questions can be anything really. I have heard questions about success in career, love, health, and so on. The seer then asks the ancestors to foretell the future. After a while, the seer comes back through the gates of Helheim and the entire congregation travels back up the world tree to the physical realm.

Solitary Oracular Seidr Rite to Ljossalfheim

The High Seat Rite of Oracular Seidr can be performed by the solitary practitioner with some alterations. The basic elements of the rite are drumming and singing yourself into a trance, journeying the world tree to your destination, speaking with the spirits about the past, present, or future, and then returning back to the physical world. In many of the High Seat Rites you typically travel into the Underworld to speak with the dead because the dead have access to the streams of time that we, the living, do not. But you can actually journey anywhere in the Nine Worlds. For our purposes with this present work, we will continue with our theme of the Otherworld and travel to speak with the elves in Ljossalfheim.

Items needed:

> At the bare minimum all you need to perform this right is you. You are the seer traveling the world tree in order to speak with the spirits. However, if you are anything like me, you may want to have some tools to help you in the process. We do not need the tools, but they are fun and add to the dramatic effect. Here are a few tools you can use to aide in your ritual.

High Seat. The high seat can be a chair or a stool. You can use anything you like that makes you feel magical. Normally, I say you can lie down to journey, but since we are doing a High Seat Right, let's try journeying sitting up. You can compare and see the difference between sitting and lying down.

Cloak. If you like you can wrap a cloak or blanket around you as you journey into Ljossalfheim. This gives you a nice "otherworldly" and magical feel. It also helps you focus inward so that you may journey easier.

Drum or rattle. It is traditional to use a drum, but you can use a rattle as well. If you are doing this alone, you will have to drum or rattle for yourself. I think a good witch or Spirit Walker should be able to drum or rattle for themselves when journeying. It may feel a bit odd at first, but you will get used to it.

Mugwort or sage. I love traveling with incense or fumigation. I love it! For a Heathen rite, it is more traditional to use mugwort, but if you do not have any you can easily use sage for the same purpose.

The High Seat Rite

1. Place your cloak or blanket around you (if you choose to use one) and sit upon the high seat.

2. Take a few moments to relax and get into a spiritual frame of mind.

3. Light your mugwort or sage and allow the smoke to rise up to fumigate the ritual space. This both banishes negative energies as well as has the aromatherapy advantage of aiding in your trance.

4. Call upon your ancestors to guard the circle. Ask them to keep out all distractions and negative energies that may inhibit your work.

5. Call upon Odin and Freya to aide and guide your ritual. Remember, Odin and Freya are the gods who brought Seidr to the people.

6. At this time, begin drumming. You may sing sacred chants if you know them or you can use vocables. Vocables are sounds like "hey hey" or "falalalala". They are words with no meaning. You add meaning with your intent. If you chose not to sing, that's ok. Continue to drum yourself into a deep trance.

7. Using one of the astral projection techniques, project your astral body to the world tree Yggdrasil. See the enormous world tree. Ask your Spirit Animal to join you. Have the intention to travel to the home of the light elves. Follow

your Spirit Animal either into the trunk of the world tree via a door, or turn around and follow the Spirit Animal. Your Spirit Animal will lead you to the Lyossalfheim.

8. Once in the Elf World, set the intention of finding an elf who is willing to take you to an Elvish Seer. When you come to the elvish seer, ask him or her what questions you may have.

9. When you are ready, thank the seer and come back to the world tree. Come back to the physical world. Take a few deep breaths and ground yourself back into this space.

10. Give an offering of some kind to the elvish seer. Remember, elves enjoy milk, bread, honey, flowers, and trinkets.

11. Give thanks to your ancestors and to Odin and Freya.

12. Journal your experience.

Chapter 5

Spirit Animals

Animal Wisdom

Animals are sacred beings who are deeply connected to the natural world. Each animal has a sacred purpose. Every life has great meaning and contributes in some way to the well-being of the earth and all of her inhabitants. Some animals help spread seeds throughout the land while other animals help break down vegetation. Predator animals keep other animal populations down. Otherwise, vegetation would be devastated. Even maggots have divine purpose. They help dead rotting flesh decompose and return to the earth. All beings upon the earth are connected to the Web of Wyrd. Each animal is connected energetically to the Universe just as we are. One of the main differences between humans and animals is that animals are true to their nature and purpose. Through evolution and adaptation, they are tuned into the cycles of the earth and her natural energies. When winter approaches, birds know to fly to warmer climates. Squirrels know to stock up food to last through the cold months and bears know to hibernate until spring. Animals do not need to be told when the earth's cycles are changing. Their energies are fine tuned to those of the earth and can feel her energy pulses. Many animals know of an upcoming storm, hurricane, or earthquake hours before we humans are aware of it.

As human beings, we are often distracted by other things than our Divine Purpose on earth. We allow other people and materialistic things to influence us into making bad decisions and sometimes even hurting ourselves. We are conflicted. More often than not, our heart is not congruent with our mind. When our hearts tell us to love our fears tell us not to. When our heart tells us to have compassion for others sometimes our ego tells us not to. Animals do not have this conflict. They are aware of their Divine Purpose and live every moment being the best they can be. The bear is 100% bear and the little crawly worm is 100% a little crawly worm. They are true to their own nature. This, I believe, is what makes animals so much wiser than us. They are connected to all things in the Universe and contribute to the earth in the very best that they can. It is through this wisdom that we can learn how to become more connected to the land and to the Universe so that we can find balance and healing within ourselves.

In our modern age, humans have come to believe that we are "above" animals and they are subjected to our Will. We use them for food, work, and entertainment. To some, they have come to be only food and slaves to us. Many times, humans see wild animals as "pests" and a danger and we hunt and kill them so that we can feel safe in the woods or any other natural environment. These same people believe that humans have a divine right to subjugate animals like this. It is my hope that anyone reading this book treat all life great or small as part of the divine. Humans are not at the top of the ecosystem nor the food chain. Humans are a part of the ecosystem and do not lead it or own it in any way. We are one part of the whole and that in itself is sacred.

Each animal has its own special gifts and powers. Every animal has a special energy that can help us heal and work magick. For example, bears are mighty in power and strength and we can learn from them how to be strong. Wolves are pack animals and they understand how to work as a group. They have the ability to teach us how to take care of our community. Hawks soar very high in the sky and can teach us how to see the big picture. Animals have many things to teach us. All we have to do is learn how to listen. In order for us to discover the energies and magick of animals we first must go out into nature and observe.

Observing Animals

We can learn many things by observing animals in their natural habitat. We can discover how they hunt or gather food, build shelter, and fend off predators. We can also observe behavior patterns and mannerisms. Simply observing animals will tell us many things about their own gifts of healing and magick.

1. Go out into a place of nature where wild animals will be. If you live in a city, you can go to a nature preserve or park.

2. Find a place where you can sit comfortably and observe your surroundings. We will need to be in a place that does not disturb the animals in any way.

3. Allow yourself to go into a light trance. You can use a modified shaking and swaying seidr technique in a sitting position. Go slower than usual. You only need to go into a slight trance for your observation.

4. Now, just be aware of the animal life that is all around you. Spend some time watching what each animal does.

5. Pay attention to how they communicate. What sounds do they make? Pay attention to how they gather food. What behavior patterns do you see? Pay attention to how they respond to other animals. Are they friendly or hostile?

6. Next, become aware of how every single animal is connected to the Web of Wyrd. Spend some time visualizing the energetic connection they have to each other and to you.

7. When you are ready to end the exercise, give thanks to the animals and leave an offering. It can be water, natural food, or just your energy.

8. Journal your experience.

Spirit Animals

Our Spirit Animal is the animal that is most connected to our spirit and our personality. Some people call the Spirit Animal our *totem* spirit. The term "totem" comes from the Ojibwe tribe who are the original inhabitants of the Northern Plains region in the United States near Michigan, Wisconsin, and Minnesota. I personally, am trying to get away from using words from Native American tribes I do not follow out of respect of that culture that I am not a part of. The reason is that many white people, especially here in the US, have a bad habit of lumping all Native American tribes into one. I, myself, have been guilty of this in my first years of learning Native traditions. When we do this, we are not honoring the difference in culture and practices and honoring the people themselves. The tribes I have been trained in are Lakota, Cherokee, and some Apache. I have learned from teachers, elders, and spiritual leaders from these communities. The Spirit Animal teachings I am presenting here are taught to me by my teachers and by the animal spirits themselves.

As human beings, we are not set apart from animals nor are we better or more evolved than our four-legged teachers. We are different than them, yes, but we are still animals. One of the lines from the HBO series *Carnivale* that has always stuck with me is that people are "crafty animals". I find this to be very true. From the beginning of time, we have associated ourselves with animals. We did this for our own spiritual healing, magick, as well as survival. Our Spirit Animal is our animal aspect of our consciousness. It is us. It is who we are. It is not some outside spirit that we call upon like when we invoke a god or goddess. The Spirit Animal is who we are. In fact, I have come to believe that the Spirit Animal is handed to us from our ancestral DNA as well as our ancestral lands. What this means is that energetically and spiritually we are linked to the animals of our ancestral lands. So, if your ancestors lived on land that contained bears, wolves, mountain lions, foxes, raccoons, and beavers, then your Spirit Animal will be one of these animals. We do not choose our Spirit Animal. We do not randomly pick an animal because we simply like it. It is a part of our being, our personality, and our heritage. Many families of the past may have had family Spirit Animals. Especially if you are European descent. I have seen many family coat of arms that had the family animal. The family Spirit Animal is not something invented in the Medieval ages, but goes back even further when we lived side by side to animals in tribal cultures.

Spirit Animals resonate with our Lower Self. The lower self is that part of our consciousness that is primal and animalistic. You could say that this is our parasympathetic system - our fight or flight aspect our ourselves. This is different from our Shadow Self that is the place of our fear and repressed memories and desires. Working with our lower self via our Spirit Animal has many benefits. By doing Spirit Animal work we are able to bring our lower self into harmony with the everyday self and the higher self. It is also a reservoir of pure untapped animal power and magick that we can use for healing and power. Spirit Animal work also helps us tap into our ancestral animal lineage that connects us to all of our ancestors. Most importantly, this work will help you connect with your animal consciousness so that you can connect more deeply to the animal world and the Earth Mother herself.

Some people already have an idea of what their animal or Spirit Animal is. There are people who have a strong affinity towards a certain animal. They may watch movies and documentaries about them, collect pictures and figurines of them, and spend time in nature looking for them. Many people are not so lucky to have this clarity. For most, we have to spend time researching our ancestral homes and animals as well as trying to understand our personality. You and your Spirit Animal will have many things in common. You will have similar behavior patterns, likes and dislikes, as well as regional preferences for your home. Whenever I have a student research their Spirit Animal, they say the same thing every single time, "This is me! I do the same things (animal) does!"

I often get the question, "Can my Spirit Animal be a bug or a bird?" Most likely, your Spirit Animal is not a bug. But in our Universe anything can happen so never say never. But usually not. What about birds. Again, this is rare but it does happen. I have seen people who have had eagle, hawk, crow, and owl as their Spirit Animal. Usually, the Spirit Animal has powerful strength, stamina, or cunning that helps it survive out in the wild. I also get the same question about domesticated animals such as a dog, cat, cow, or pig. I have heard many Spirit Walkers say that you cannot be a domesticated animal because they gave up their primal nature in favor of humans. I would like to take a look at this silly notion for a moment. If you have ever seen a dog attack someone in defence of their owner then you have seen they have not given up their primal nature. My cat Azreal, is spoiled rotten at home. She is the Queen of the house! She is fed her favorite foods and is getting fat. That being said, if she sees a bug, or heaven forbid a mouse, she changes into "The Huntress" and the critter must die. This is why she is named Azreal. I have come to understand that domesticated animals have chosen to be our animal friends, healers, guides, and counselors. They did not give up their nature but chose to help us as valued animal partners in life. As a human race, I have come to believe that we need them more than they need us.

Finding Your Spirit Animal

In order to find your Spirit Animal, you are going to go on a spirit journey. I like to take students into a deep dark forest to find the Spirit Animal. The reason I prefer the deep forest is because in our western mindset, the forests is full of a variety of animals. Almost everyone has been in a forest or at least a patch of woods before. Not everyone has been to a desert or mountain range. The other reason is that psychologically, the dark forest is symbolic for the deep subconscious mind where we can find our Spirit Animal. As you journey into the primal forest of the Midworld, you are also journeying into your deep mind. This is one of the things I love about Spirit Walking. You simultaneously traveling into the Otherworld and your mind! The animals that you find do not have to be forest animals. You can find ANY animal in the forest of the Otherworld. But, if you really feel that you want to journey into the grassy plains of Africa, the jungles of South America, or the Deserts of the United States, trust your intuition. This is not a hard and fast rule. In fact, most "rules" in Spirit Walking should be altered to fit your needs and the advice of the spirits.

1. Refer to one of the astral projection/journeying techniques from Chapter 2.
2. Once you are in the Otherworld, visualize yourself at the World Tree. See its giant trunk that seems to go on for miles in either direction. Look up into the sky and see the mighty branches that go deep into the cosmos. Look at the great roots of the tree and see how they go down deep into the center of the earth.
3. Turn around so that your back is facing the World Tree. You see before you an ancient forest that is thousands and thousands of years old. This forest is thick and dark and no sunlight penetrates through the thick tree branches. You can hear the sounds of the wind moving the branches as well as many animals and birds singing their medicine songs in the wild forest.
4. Begin walking along the little path that is before you. With each step you walk deeper and deeper into the forests. The air smells of the fragrance of trees that have been here almost as long as time itself.
5. State your intention to find your Spirit Animal. Open your heart chakra and be open to the experience. Continue to walk deeper and deeper into the forest. With your open

heart, reach out energetically to your Spirit Animal. Call to your Spirit Animal with your heart as you would a long-lost friend or loved one.

6. As you walk further into the forest, you know that you are being watched by many animals and birds.

7. Do any of the animals come to you or cross your path?

8. If so, send a beam of energy with your heart chakra and ask the animal if it is your Spirit Animal. Spend a moment or two with it and see what is says. You will be able to understand the language of animals in the Otherworld.

9. If it says "Yes," then you have found your Spirit Animal. If no, then keep walking on the path. Sometimes, animals that cross our path want to be animal helpers. This is great. Take note of this and revisit this later. You will know this is your Spirit Animal because it will feel like a homecoming. Like you are coming home to yourself. This experience will feel joyful and full of healing.

10. When you have found your Spirit Animal, ask him/ her to energetically combine with your aura and your physical body. The Spirit Animal is already apart of you. This technique is to remind your conscious self about your Spirit Animal.

11. When you come back to your body, journal your experience.

If you do not find you Spirit Animal during this journey, that is OK. You will take this journey every day until you find it.

Ecstatic Dancing With Your Spirit Animal

After you have discovered your Spirit Animal, you should perform an ecstatic dance with them. Dancing with your Spirit Animal will help both of you get reacquainted with each other both on the physical level as well as the energetic and astral levels.

1. Use the Trance Dance technique in Chapter 3.
2. Once you have achieved a trance state call upon your Spirit Animal with your heart chakra. Bring the energies of your Spirit Animal into your heart. Take a deep breath and breathe these energies out in front of you. Visualize your Spirit Animal in front of you as clearly as possible.
3. Visualize your Spirit Animal dancing with you. See them doing ecstatic dance alongside you. Each animal has their own dance. Allow them to dance as they will. Sometimes you will even see them copying our movements!
4. Feel the animal power emanating from them. Breathe this power into your body.
5. Take a breath and send them energy as well. Continue sharing dance and energy throughout the whole dance.
6. When you are ready, breathe in your Spirit Animal back into your body.
7. Journal your experience. Feel free to dance with your Spirit Animal any time you like. This is a great healing technique as well.

Spirit Animal Magick

There is very powerful magick you can do with your Spirit Animal. Anytime you journey into any of the three worlds you should have your Spirit Animal with you. They are your most powerful protector against danger or any entity that wishes you harm. During journeys, if I find myself in a dangerous place, my Spirit Animal will pull me away. You will have a psychic link to them and you will know when they are sensing danger. They will also attack any spirit who is trying to attack you. Do not be surprised to see the gentle doe becoming a fierce protector when you are attacked!

Your Spirit Animal will help you learn to understand the animal kingdom in a deep personal way. The more you work with your Spirit Animal the more you will be attuned to the natural world and all of her inhabitants. You may also notice that when this happens, animals will become more comfortable with you. Squirrels will not run away at the first sight of you. Birds will seem to be singing to you. Also, dogs and cats will come right up to you. I cannot tell you how many times someone who was walking their dog said to me, "That's strange! She never goes right up to people and jumps on them! She must really like you."

Your Spirit Animal can help you with strength and healing. If you feel threatened, your Spirit Animal will immediately come to your rescue through your body. You may feel a hundred times stronger and more focused when in danger. When you are sick or hurt, your Spirit Animal has the ability to heal you at a much faster rate than the normal human rate. Animals in the wild heal much quicker than humans. They have to. As humans, we have our comforts and the luxury of spending time in bed or in a cast until we are fully healed. If an animal is hurt, they do not get to rest for too long. To do so would risk getting hurt by predators and starvation. It is necessary for them to heal faster. When you call upon your Spirit Animal either in ecstatic dance, shaking and swaying seidr, or meditation and journeys, they will help you heal at a much faster rate.

Animal Helpers

In February of 2011, I spent a week in Palm Springs, California with my friend Tom. We spent a day hiking up the mountain and walking through the beautiful desert nature preserve. There were many lizards and birds all over the place. This particular nature preserve was said to be governed by a Native American spiritual leader who was banished from the community for doing black magick. Who knows if it is true, but it is a fun story. I spent some time there hiking up and down the mountain. There were two crows that flew in the sky above. Everywhere I went there were these same two crows. Many times, I would walk through the hills in Palm Springs that week. Every single time, those two crows were flying overhead near me. I could sense the spiritual connection. That April, I traveled to Sedona, Arizona to work with a Native American spiritual leader to help me make my Chanupa; the sacred pipe. He taught me how to make the pipe bowl and the stem in a sacred manner. Making a chanupa by hand takes many days to complete and I was only there for one weekend. So, I took my chanupa home to complete. When I got home, I unwrapped the cloth around the chanupa and began working on it. I took a metal file and filed down the pipe stone. I began to hear squawking sounds! They were so loud! The noise was coming from my bedroom. When I went to my bedroom, I saw a large crow standing in my window. He looked right at me and squawked very loudly again. Ah, I told myself, this is Crow medicine. Crow has much to teach me about its medicine and the chanupa. Crow is now one of my animal helpers. I now have a tattoo of Crow on my upper shoulders.

All animals are sacred and holy. They have much to teach of us about the world and how we can find balance and healing. I have come to believe that each animal is a divine thread in the Web of Wyrd. Each of them is an important part of the intricate tapestry that is the Web. They each have a sacred purpose and they can teach us many things as well as share their powers with us. By studying animals in nature, we can see what gifts each one possesses. Foxes are very cunning. Horses run at great speeds. Mountain Lions are skilled hunters. Every animal has wonderful powers. It is not the size of the animal, but what it is able to do. In energy healing and Spirit Walking, we can ask animals to be our helpers and to aide us when we need. One of my other animal helpers is the hare. Hare is connected to the growth of the earth and fertility. Hare also speeds along the forest when it needs to. When I ask for Hare to help me, Hare teaches me about the life cycle of the earth. Hare also teaches me to use caution around people I do not know. Hare is always watching; very alert to all possible dangers.

You may have many different animal helpers during your life. You can also have several helpers at the same time. Animal helpers are different than your Spirit Animal in that your Spirit Animal is YOU and you only get one your entire life. Animal helpers are different in that regard. You may have several and they may come and go as they chose. It is very beneficial to the Spirit Walker and witch to work with animal helpers. They can give you healing power when you are healing yourself and others. They also will give you messages from The Creator and the Web of Wyrd. I have learned that when Crow comes to me with a message, it is usually something that is happening with Fate and the Great Mystery. Crow has these powers, so naturally this is what Crow wants to tell me about. Another animal helper I have is Snake. May patron deity is Aesculapius, the Greco-Roman god of healing, and he carries a staff that a red snake has curled around. This is actually where we get the caduceus from-the medical symbol. So naturally, Snake is one of my animal helpers that helps me in healing ceremonies. Snake will often come into the ceremony and slither on to the client and eat the disease. The client is almost always unaware of Snake and his healing powers in the ceremony so I never worry about him accidentally given someone a fright.

Lately, I have been seeing many books and groups on social media teach that each time you see an animal it has a special meaning just for us. Not to be harsh, but this way of thinking is human arrogance. It is true that we are all connected, but not everything is a special meaning for us. Remember, we are a part of the Web of Wyrd and not the center of it. We are no more or less important to the Universe than any other animal. Sometimes, the Universe *does* send us personal messages, like Crow who came to my bedroom window or when we are doing ceremony. When a wild animal seems to go out of their way to come up to you, odds are this is a message from the Universe. Another way to tell if there is a message for you is if you see an animal that you do not usually see in your area. Once, when I was on my way to work, I saw a falcon watching me as I came out the door of my building. Falcon had something to say. The best way to be able to tell if an animal helper has messages for you is to constantly work with animals in your ceremonies and healing practices. When doing any kind of outdoor ceremony, invite the animals to attend. Some may come. Some will not. But rest assured that many animals will keep hidden as they watch you honor the earth and the old gods.

Finding An Animal Helper

Some of the most powerful healing comes from animal helpers. Some helpers may have already made themselves known and you. Are there any animals that you have a connection with or an affinity for? I have a friend who loves frogs. If you go into his home there are frog pictures, figurines, and statues. He really loves them. That is a definite sign that Frog is one of his helpers. Are there any animals that you are kind of obsessed with? I have an infatuation with sharks. I think they are the coolest thing and I watch every shark documentary I can get my hands on. So, yes, shark is one my helpers. Are there any animals that keep showing up anytime you go out in nature? Do squirrels seem to follow you around? Is there a red cardinal that comes to or near you every time you are in a wooded area? That is a wonderful sign that that is an animal helper.

If you are unsure who your animal helpers are you can do a short ceremony to ask the Universe to send you an animal helper. You will need a food offering of some kind, sage, cedar, or some other herbs to burn, a fireproof container, and water.

1. Go out into a natural area.
2. Give an offering of water. You can place it on a large rock or a bowl that is either biodegradable or made of natural materials that you will retrieve at a later time.

3. Light your herb and smudge yourself. Allow the herb to burn in a fireproof container, Breath in the aromatherapy properties.

4. Allow yourself to go into a light trance. Expand your aura to encompass the environment around you. Connect to the Web of Wyrd.

5. Pick up the fireproof container with the smoking herb. Say out loud a simple prayer asking for The Creator to send you an animal helper. State your reasons why you need the animal helper. For example, tell Creator you need to learn, healing, magick, spiritual growth, etc.

6. Spend some time observing nature. Watch the wind blowing through the trees. Listen to the sound of birds and animals moving through bushes.

7. Open your heart chakra and send love to all of nature and all animals.

8. Take notice if any animal comes near you. It could be animal or bird. If an animal does come to you spend some time connecting with it. Send the energy of love through your heart chakra to the animal. Try not to make any sudden moves so you do not scare it off. Ask the animal if it would like to be a helper.

9. When you are ready, end the ceremony and leave the food offering.

10. If no animal comes up to you, that is ok. They may make themselves known at a later time. Pay attention to the next few days and see if an animal crosses your path or otherwise makes themselves known to you. Sometimes your animal helper will make itself known to you through dreams or subsequent journeys. However they make themselves known is perfectly fine.

Animal Healing

All animals on the earth have something to teach us if we are open to their powers of healing. When we are open to the energies of animals, we will be able to heal and find balance from their wisdom. Just as I stated earlier, all beings upon the earth are connected to the Web of Wyrd. Animals influence the Universe just as we influence the Universe. Each animal has its own special gifts and powers. There are many stories about animals using their natural gifts to teach us about ourselves and the world around us. These stories and legends are used as teaching tools to show us the nature of the animals as well as give examples of how to handle (or how not to handle) a situation. Every animal has a special energy that can help us heal. It is believed that the Creator gave each animal special gifts and abilities in order to live and be happy upon the earth. The Native American people call this energy "medicine". Medicine, from a Native American point of view, is the energy that brings us back into balance with all things. This balance will help us heal from our physical, emotional, mental, and spiritual wounds. For example, Bear, has the medicine of strength and healing. When we observe Bear in the wild, we see that she has very powerful strength when she needs to defend herself or her cubs. Bear also can be observed digging up medicine roots with her claws. Elk medicine is that of love. Elk walks through the forest with much grace and when in danger the male Elk will fiercely protect female Elk from harm. Many of the Native American tribes, such as the Lakota and Cherokee, will pray to Eagle. Eagle can be observed flying very high in the sky. Eagle flies the highest of all birds so, therefore, is closer to the Creator. Eagle has a powerful eye and can see prey from way high in the sky and swoop down and grab it up in its mighty talons. With these observations, Eagle medicine is that of leadership, power, spirituality, and healing. When we observe the turtle, we can see that it lives both in water and on dry land. It also uses its own shell for shelter and protection against predators. Because of this observation, Turtle is a very magical creature. It has the medicine to go into our physical world as well as the Spirit World. This is one of the reasons turtle shells can be used as rattles to help us travel into the spirit world. Crow is very sacred medicine. When Crow travels in groups they are called a "murder of crows". They are very intelligent and have a strong memory. They are scavengers and eat dead things as well. They are a beautiful black color with black beaks and have an air of mystery. Their voices are not the beautiful bird song like Robin. Because of these observations, Crow has the medicine of mystery, death, and the Spirit World. We call upon Crow medicine to help us guide our way through the Otherworld and when we wish to call spirits to us. Mouse has the energies of detail and survival. Mouse is often hunted by predators so they have a powerful sense of survival. Also, because of the size of Mouse, she is able to see the detail in all things. Each animal has medicine and knowledge to teach us. When we pay attention, we can listen to the messages that Spirit has for each of us.

The Witch's Familiar

In Traditional Witchcraft, the witch's familiar is a magical being that helps us with our magick. The familiar can be a chthonic spirit, an ancestor, or an animal spirit. During the witch trials, it was believed that the Devil gave the witch a demon in the form of an animal that performed the witch's bidding. The Christians believed that the animal, or imp, would suck at the witch's teat that was hidden somewhere on the witch's body. During the physical examination, witch hunters would look for this teat as proof of guilt of the witch. In reality, if found this was not teat that the animal would suckle, but rather a skin abnormality as a mole or skin tag. Witch hunters believed that any creature that was nocturnal or exotic was proof that its owner was sure to be a witch. The common animals linked to witchcraft were the cat, frog, mouse, bird, ferret, owl, bat, spider and many others.

In the Traditional Craft that I belong to, the animal familiar is an animal helper spirit that helps in many forms of magick. The main difference between a witch's familiar and the animal helper of a Spirit Walker is that witches have a deep spiritual connection to our familiar and we usually have just one whereas the Spirit Walker can have several animal helpers. We sometimes send our familiar out to find out information for us from very far away. We also can send healing energy to someone through them. We can also use them to magically influence a situation or event if we need. The familiar is given to us at the point of initiation into traditional craft or we can ask the horned god, sometimes referred to as The Devil or The Master, to send us one. The familiar is our link to the animal world. It makes sense that the Horned One would send as an animal spirit because one of his aspects is the master of the wild wood.

Animals in Ceremonial Tools

We will have many magical and spiritual tools that will aid us in witchcraft and Spirit Walking. All of our tools should be made from natural materials. We walk an earth-based spiritual path after all. Many of our tools are made from animals. This is because we are asking the powers and healing abilities of these animals to help us in our ceremonies. If we look to the Lakota people, we will see that when they use an animal, such as the buffalo, for food they do not waste one single thing. The meat, of course is used for food, while the rest of the animal is used for everyday tools as well as magical tools. There are many parts of an animal that is used such as skin, bones, hooves, horns, teeth, bladder, shells, as well as many other things. When an animal is killed the great spirit of the animal is prayed to and offerings are given. We always pray to the animal and give it much respect and honor before it is used for our own purposes. There are many tools you can use in witchcraft and Spirit Walking. Here are some of the most common ones.

Drums

Traditional drums are made with animal skin. The skin can be bison, elk, deer, or cow. The frame itself is made from wood and represents the plant kingdom. Drums are the heartbeat of Mother Earth and the healing powers of the animal used is brought into ceremonies. Drums amplify the healing energy that the ceremonial leader sends into the drum.

Rattles

Rattles made from animals are usually those with a shell such as turtles and tortoises. These animals have very powerful healing medicine. Turtles can represent the earth itself. They also have the ability to swim as well as crawl on the earth so turtles teach us how to go between the worlds.

Staffs

Staffs are usually made from a tree branch but has animal parts fastened to it. There is no hard and fast way you must create your staff, but some spiritual traditions have a certain way to create a staff depending upon how it is used. Many healers put deer antlers or other animal horns upon the staff. Sometimes they may attach fur, shells, bones, and other things to harness the animal medicine they wish to use. I personally, have a dried snake attached to my healing staff that is dedicated to Asclepius.

Bags

Some of the bags we use are made from animal skin. They are used to carry sacred herbs and tools. I have a large bag made from animal skin that is used to keep my chanupa (sacred pipe). I have smaller bags that I use to keep sacred herbs such as tobacco, sage, cedar, and sweet grass.

Bones

The bones of an animals represent the pure spirit of an animal.

When an animal dies, it sheds its physical body and only its spirit remains. When we observe the process of decay, we see that the physical body of an animal rots back into the earth and only the bones remain. With this in mind, bones represent the spirit since both remain intact upon death. Witches and Spirit Walkers use bones to channel the healing medicine of that animal into ceremonies. Bones are added to tools or are tools themselves in order to better call upon the energies of the animal.

Shells

Shells are used to decorate tools, place in rattles to make the shaking sound, or can be used to hold smudge and fumigations. I have an abalone shell that I use to burn sacred herbs for purifications, blessings, and offerings for the spirits.

Healing and Power Necklaces

One of the things that are very powerful to Spirit Walkers is using animal parts for healing and power that are used in necklaces. Some Native Americans call these things *medicine bags*. Many earth-based cultures from around the globe use natural materials such as herbs, stones, and animal materials for magick and healing. We can use anything from animal skin, teeth, claws, bones, feathers and sometimes animal organs. When we use an animal part as a necklace, we are summoning the energies of the animal to mix with our own energies of our chakras, meridians, and our aura. For example, we could use bear claws for both healing and strength. Using animal energies to help heal and empower is one of the most sacred uses for the animal spirit.

Chapter 6

Shapeshifting

"He was the greatest eagle dancer our tribe ever had. Watching him you forgot that it was a man dancing, not a bird. He spoke about this: 'I was great doing the eagle dance. I could make myself into Wanbli, the sacred bird. I could think and move like a bird, move slowly, cock my head, turn it this way and that way-just like an eagle...The eagle has to soar, to fly high. I could crawl into the mind of an eagle. An eagle spirit took over my body.' Father's dance was a prayer, a sacredness."
Crow Dog, *Crow Dog: Four Generations of Sioux Medicine Men*

Shapeshifting is one of the most powerful techniques of animal magick. There are stories from around the world of people changing into animal form. Central Europe has many stories of men turning into werewolves during the full moon. In the U.S., the Algonquin tribe has the story of the *wendigo.* The legend of the wendigo says that during cold winter nights, anyone who is so hungry that they engage in cannibalism is cursed to transform into the half man half beast who forever haunts the forest to feast on human flesh. In Japan, there is the Kitsune, a magical fox who can shapeshift into human form. Most kitsune are simply mischievous, but some are troublesome; leading some humans to their death. There are also the stories of witches who can transform into animals and fly off to the sabbat so that they may dance with the devil and perform magick.

Shapeshifting has been found in many places from around the world. Those who possess the ability to change into animal form are very powerful and even feared. When we encounter people who are connected with the land and follow earth-based religious traditions we find that they use shapeshifting for spiritual growth and the betterment of the people. When we look at cultures who are patriarchal, we see that shapeshifting into animals is feared and often in league with darker powers. Shapeshifting is a powerful technique that we can use to connect to animals on a very deep meaningful level. By using these magnificent animal powers, you can summon forth the energies of healing, transformation, spiritual growth, magick, protection, and the well-being of the community as a whole.

The Native American people see animals as expressions of the divine presence of the Universe and the Creator. Each animal has their own powers that enables them to contribute to the betterment of the tribe and the earth itself. Many Native American dances incorporate shapeshifting elements. The Lakota had several different Buffalo dances. Each of the dances had a different purpose. Some of the Buffalo dances were dances of thanks and gratitude. Others were meant to call upon the power of buffalo. While other dances were meant to call the Buffalo near so that the tribe would have a good hunt. Often times, the dancers would dress with buffalo skins and paint so that they may connect to the Buffalo in a deep and profound way. In their book, *Indian Dances of North America,* Reginald and Gladys Laubin said:

> "In all of them (dances) there were some dancers dressed as buffalo, with great headdresses-sometimes a complete mask-of buffalo hide and horns. Often these headdresses included a strip of fur that extended all the way to the tail, worn down the dancer's back."

The Yaqui tribe, located in Arizona have the Deer dance. The dance is performed to call upon the deer medicine that could cure the sick and grant good hunting. The Deer dancer places a deer head upon a cap that he wears on his head and makes dancing movements that is similar to the behavior of dear such as jumping, prancing, and various head movements that a deer would make. Many of the tribes of North American had an Eagle Dance. The Eagle has medicine of spiritual growth, healing, and power. The Shawnees' Eagle Dance is performed to honor the sacredness of Eagle. It is interesting because, not only do they carry eagle feathers, but the dance depicts the behaviors of the Eagle such as using the mouth to pick things up.

Many animals have great strength, power, and healing abilities. When we connect to the energies of animals and call them into our bodies, we can harness this animal power within ourselves. By observing animals in the wild we can see how truly powerful they are. Cheetahs are the fastest creatures on the planet going up to speeds of 75 miles per hour. Bears have incredible strength and can tear a person limb from limb. Lions have the ability to heal from wounds at an incredible pace so therefore are powerful healers. Throughout history indigenous people have been summoning the powers of animals in order to help the people of the tribe. One of the most famous examples of this is the depiction of indigenous person in the caves of Les Trois Freres. This is a cave painting of a man which seems to be either dressed in the skin of an animal or he has shapeshifted into an animal. We really do not know the purpose of this painting but we can guess it may have been a painting of someone who is magically calling out to the animal for a good hunt or even, perhaps, it was depicting someone harnessing the powers of the animal. The Berserkers are a warrior tribe in Northern Europe that shapeshift into bears during battle. Berserker means "bear shirt" and they were known to wear bear hides in order to shapeshift into the ferocious bear during battle. When this happened, the Berserker would go so deep into bear consciousness that Bear would take over and the warrior would gain incredible strength and power to defeat their enemies. Witches are also known to shapeshift as well.

In Traditional Witchcraft, there are elements of shamanism

that are the core of our practice. Witches, like shamans and Spirit Walkers, have the ability to go into ecstatic trance, journey in the spirit, work with animal helpers, as well as change into the shape of animals. Emma Wilby in her book *Cunning Folk and Familiar Spirits: Shamanistic Visionary Traditions in Early Modern British Witchcraft and Magic* says:

"Several sabbath accounts from this period (16th-17th Century) also describe 'animal metamorphosis', that is, the changing of a human into animal form, a process which could also occur outside the sabbath. Renfrewshire witch Marie Lamont (1662), for example claimed that at the end of the sabbath she and her companions changed into animal form in order to be able to perform maleficent magic".

In some Traditional Witchcraft circles, there are the shapeshifting masks rites. During the ritual, witches will put on animal masks and through ecstatic trance and energy raising techniques they would transform their energies and minds into that of the animal in order to honor the spirits and the animal itself. Evan John Jones and Chas S. Clifton in their book *Sacred Mask Sacred Dance* said:

"By going to the rite and putting on the mask and then joining the circle dance, one particular member had gone into the ecstatic trance-like dance where this world ceased to exist for him and where he met the spirit of the god of the animal whose mask he was wearing. During the dance he would have felt a kinship with the animal, thought of himself as an animal, and in his own mind, become the animal."

Shapeshifting is a very powerful technique that can enhance your magical and healing practice. We can learn to have a deeper relationship with our own personal Spirit Animal and by doing so we can learn how to incorporate its energies into our healing rituals and ceremonies. This is very similar to invoking the gods. In my book *Upperworld: Shamanism and Magic of the Celestial Realm,* I talk about how the most intimate ways to experience the gods and connect with them is through deity invocation. During invocation, you summon the energies of the god or goddess into your energy and physical body. By doing this, we share our thoughts, our desires, our emotions, and our bodies. To me, this is the highest form of devotion. The essence of devotion is energy exchange be it by prayers, offerings, or the actual exchange of energies. The entire time you are invoking a deity you are exchanging energies. The god is nourished from these energies that are emanating from your body. Benefits of sharing energies with the gods include magical power, healing, oracles, and spiritual evolution. There is a similar energy exchange when we are shapeshifting to our Spirit Animal. I want to reiterate that when we shapeshift into our Spirit Animal it is not an outside entity. It is a part of our own being. Our own consciousness. When we are in animal form we are connecting to the great spirit of our animal. My Spirit Animal is the mountain lion. When I shapeshift into him, I am connecting to the great Mountain Lion. I am learning about his behaviors, instincts, physical abilities and defences. I am also learning about his energies, magical abilities, and his healing medicines that he shares with the world.

Animal Consciousness

In order for us to truly connect with animals for magick, healing, and shapeshifting, it is vital that we connect with animal consciousness. By doing so, we are able to more fully understand the mental functions, energies, emotions, and physical wants and needs of animals. People who want to fully understand another person try to connect with their way of thinking. This has the benefit of helping that person understand why they feel a certain way about a subject and gives them insight into their decision-making process. When we understand someone's mentality, it is much easier to have a dialogue with them. A wise leader cannot make decisions for their people without knowing the needs and wants of the people. If we use this philosophy with shapeshifting and animal magick, it will be much easier to tune into the energies and mental functions of the animal so that we can truly connect with them for magick.

It is easier to understand animal consciousness than you might think. We have all heard people say that we are animals. This is very true; we are mammals. But it goes far beyond that. Let us take a look at the evolution of our brain and how it is connected to animals. This explanation is admittedly over simplified about the evolution of life, but will serve to give you the basic idea of the evolution of the human brain. Paul D. Maclean was a neuroscientist who came up with the idea of the *triune brain.* The triune brain says that our brains are divided into three parts: the reptilian brain, the limbic system, and the neocortex. When life first came out of the ocean and crawled upon the earth these amphibians, and later reptiles, had what is commonly known as the *reptilian brain.* The reptilian brain is concerned with survival of self and species. This part of the brain controls the functions of hunger, aggression, moving, and sexual reproduction as well as social dominance. It also regulates the bodies survival functions necessary for life.

Through millions of years of evolution, mammals began to roam the earth. With evolution of mammals came the evolution of the limbic system which grew around the reptilian brain. The limbic system contains the amygdala. The amygdala is an almond shaped part of the brain that regulates emotions. This is important because this is where we get the emotions of rage, fear, and care of our young. Mammals base their responses on the input of emotions. For example, if a small animal is being chased by prey, the fear response kicks in and it runs for its life. If an animal is being attacked, then the rage response kicks in and it is able to defend itself. Both these examples show the importance of strong "animal" emotions. The importance of animal emotions cannot be overstressed. Each animal takes in emotions and its response to them based on its interaction with the environment around them. Sarah-Keena Koch in her online article "Brain Evolution -The Triune Brain Theory" http://mybrainnotes.com/evolution-brain-maclean.html says, "You have to remember here that a rabbit's world is much different than a chimpanzee's world or a human's world. Every mammal has its own world view to speak."

After many more years of evolution, the neocortex grew around the limbic system. The neocortex is responsible for taking information from the environment by touch, sight, and hearing. Through these senses, this area of the brain produces deductive reasoning. It is also the place where we get our language. Animals such as primates, whales, and dolphins have a neocortex function that is similar to ours while most other mammals have a very limited neocortex. Humans are not the only species to have deductive reasoning. Many animals have been found to have reasoning. We know this with the stereotypical scientific experiment that involves a mouse searching a maze for cheese. We use all these areas of the brain. Each of them is a major development in our brains evolutionary process and each of them function very differently and processes information differently. This information is important to us for shapeshifting and animal magick is because by understanding the "animal" functions of the brain/mind, we are able to connect with this way of thinking and understanding the interactions animals have with the world and with themselves.

Now that we have a very general idea of the different areas of the brain, including the "mammalian brain" of the limbic system, let us take a look at animal consciousness. Consciousness is said to be the thought process of being awake and observing things around the person or animal as well as being aware. "Aware" being the thought process of understanding what is happening to you in the environment that you are in. Each species of animal has *innate behavior*. This is a behavior pattern in a species of an animal as a whole that does not have to be learned or taught. Some people call this behavior *instinct.* Innate behaviors can be seen in many animals. For example, a squirrel does not have to be taught to climb a tree and eat nuts. Another innate behavior is when a bird automatically knows how to hunt for food and build nests. It has been shown that these behaviors are developed because of some need. Most commonly the need is food, but can be for protection and shelter.

When we are trying to understand the consciousness of an animal, one way is through a term called *phenomenal consciousness* which occurs when we have direct experience of something. So, in the case of shapeshifting, it will help us a great deal if we have an idea what it is like to be that animal directly. Since, most of us have never been an animal before in this life we have to imagine what it would be like through a similar experience. For example, we can imagine what it is like to be a wolf. We can close our eyes and visualize ourselves being a wolf and doing wolf things, but with phenomenal consciousness we must go out in nature, live in a pack, howl at the moon and hunt prey. Even with all of this we cannot be 100% sure what it is to be like to be a wolf. What we are able to do in this point of our magical development with animals is to observe and try to understand their nature and how their minds work. We know that animals have emotions. We see that our dogs are excited to see us when we get home from work and may be frightened by a thunderstorm. When we observe animals in nature, we see that many of the emotions that they display are those of aggression, anger, and fear; at least towards us as humans. These are considered primal emotions because they are important for the survival of animals. We also know that animals show affection towards each other much like a momma bear having a bond with her cubs. Some people have said this connection is nothing more than instinct and is not an indicator of love or a family bond. When we spend a lot of time with animals, both domestic and wild, we see that this is not the case. Animals show love, attachment and bonding towards other creatures.

We also know that animals communicate with each other. A mother duck knows the sounds of her ducklings. In fact, most animal mothers know the voice of their young. Animals communicate in many other ways as well. We know that humpback whales communicate with whale song than be heard by other humpbacks for up to 10,000 miles in the ocean. Scientists believe the songs are meant for breeding. I believe the songs are much more than this. In many Native American cosmologies, Whales are the record keepers of the earth. This makes sense because they are known to swim thousands of miles. I believe that these songs are part of the stories that whales tell one another. When an animal feels threatened, they will growl and show their teeth. This is done to tell the other animals that they are threatened in some way, or perhaps guarding territory, and to continue on their current path is to invite a dreadful fight.

Animal consciousness is far more than just the survival of an animal or reproduction. Animals show a variety of emotions as well such as compassion and curiosity. Crows are known to bring back rewards to people who feed them. BBC.com news posted an article back in February of 2015 about a little girl in Seattle, Washington, who fed crows daily. The little girl, Gabi Mann, would feed the crows table scraps, peanuts, and dog food. The crows would gather each day waiting for a meal. Then, the crows began giving Gabi little trinkets of pieces of metal, Lego, plastic items, and sometimes jewelry that they had found to show their gratitude. We also know of dolphins who have protected people out in the ocean from shark attack. In the year 2000 a man named Kevin Hines jumped off the Golden Gate Bridge in San Francisco to commit suicide. Miraculously, Kevin survived the fall into the cold ocean waters. A sea lion had saw the jump and came to Kevin's rescue. She kept Kevin afloat until the Coast Guard was able to rescue him. In 1996, a boy named Rheal Guindon, from Ontario, Canada witnessed his parents boat tip over on a camping trip drowning them. Rheal attempted to walk back to town but night fell and the temperature dropped to below freezing. Rheal, orphaned and alone, went to sleep on the cold ground only to awaken to see that three beavers had cuddled next to him all night long in order to keep him warm.

Animal consciousness is not as cut and dry as we once thought in our Western society. Animals have very complex thoughts and behaviors that astonish us and keep us in awe. They may have a brain function that we once thought was simpler than ours but it turns out that they are an enigma that we are still trying to figure out today. Many tribal cultures such as Native American Lakota, the Shamans of Siberia, and the Bushman of South Africa have known that the consciousness of animals is tuned into the natural world as well as the world of spirit that is around us all.

Research

The first thing you will want to do for shapeshifting is do some research with your chosen animal. You will need to know where your Spirit Animal lives naturally. This will tell you what kind of environment that it will navigate through on a day to day basis. It will also tell you the different seasons it has to adapt to. For example, there are many different types of bears that live around the world. If we do some research and want to understand Grizzly Bears, specifically, we will want to understand where they live, what they eat, how they move around their environment, and how they defend themselves. Using this example, I would recommend that you read a few books on the nature of Grizzly Bears. If you do a quick Google search you will find many things. On https://defenders.org/grizzly-bear/basic-facts I was able to find all the quick information I needed to start my research. Now, this is only a quick article and it is important that you do some in-depth research so that you can better understand Grizzly Bear. Doing research on your Spirit Animal will help you a great deal when it comes to shapeshifting as well as working magically with your animal. The more you understand it, the more powerful your connection will be.

Observation

Ideally, you will need to observe your animal in nature. By observing your Spirit Animal, we can see how it moves and how it relates to other animals as well as its environment. When the Lakota observed bears, they noticed that she would sniff out roots and then dig them up and eat them. Some of the Lakota healers would follow them and find the roots bears had dug up and use them in healing. This is one of the reasons why the Bear is called upon to help in healing ceremonies. Also, by observing Grizzly Bears we can see how they are very protective of their bear cubs and they are very powerful creatures. When they feel threatened, they stand on their hind legs and growl. This is only a small pinch of Grizzly Bear behavior, but I wanted to give you an idea of how observation can help you understand behaviors.

Many times, observing our Spirit Animal in nature is not possible because we live in cities. It can also be dangerous to observe some animals in nature. I, for one, would not want to get anywhere near a Grizzly Bear out in the forest. My Spirit Animal is the Mountain Lion and I would hope that he would recognize a kindred spirit in nature, but Mountain Lions are territorial and they may view me as a threat and attack to protect their home. Living in the 21st Century, we have the luxury of watching videos online of animal behavior. This helps us a great deal because we are able to watch videos of our Spirit Animal's behavior in the wild without causing harm to ourselves and, most importantly, to the animal. Humans have destroyed so much of nature that many habitats have been destroyed or greatly reduced. We should not cause any more damage than we already have.

What about zoos? This is a controversial topic. On one hand, because habitats have been destroyed, animals have nowhere to go, so some people think zoos are necessary for animal survival. With this thinking, it is far better to build an animal sanctuary for animals. This will keep them out of cages and out of display to people who see them as entertainment and not the spiritual creatures that they are. Then there is the other hand that says for many people, without zoos we would never have the opportunity to see many animals in real life. There is a point to this statement, but this is a very selfish "human" thing to do. It is more important for the animals to be safe and happy than for us to visit them. Even if we love them, we are making it about us and not about the needs and wants of the animals. Personally, I think that if we would rebuild animal habitats and revitalize nature we would have no need for zoos at all.

If you decide to visit a zoo to commune and observe with your Spirit Animal then we should give them healing energy. Observing an animal in a zoo will not teach you about its behavior. Many times, animals are caged and depressed and are not very active. They are fed daily and do not have to hunt for food. If you visit a zoo, I would recommend giving the animal healing energy for well-being and happiness. If you choose, you can connect to the great spirit of the animal by sending love energy from your spirit to the animal's spirit. So, if I want to commune with the great Bear spirit, I would send a beam of energy from my spirit to the bear's spirit. Then I would share my thoughts and emotions with Bear and ask if Bear wanted anything from me. Then I would send healing energy to bear in the zoo. There are many other things you can do besides send bear energy. You can donate your time and/or money to causes that seek to preserve natural habitats of animals.

Placing Your Consciousness Into An Animal

Another way to get to know an animal for shapeshifting is to place your consciousness into the consciousness of an animal. This is similar to invoking a spirit into your body, but instead we will send our mind into the mind of an animal. It is very important that you get the animals permission first before you do this. You would not want a spirit jumping into your mind so we would never do that to an animal without first getting permission. Animals are our teachers and we always treat them with the utmost respect and reverence. By joining your mind with an animal, you will get a very unique perspective. You will have access to the animal's thoughts, emotions, and energies. For this exercise, we only want to observe. The animal will, of course, know we are in their mind, but we are not to control them or interfere with their daily routine. We are only there to learn a deeper understanding of the animal.

When performing this technique go out into nature where your spirit animal is likely to be. Sit quietly and wait for your animal to come by. If they do not come, you can focus on your heart chakra and send out a call to them. Ask them to come to you so you may learn from them. You can use this technique for any animal you would like a better understanding of.

1. Place yourself into a trance space. You can use ecstatic dance, shaking and swaying seidr, or any trance technique you prefer. If you are being cautious of not disturbing the animal, you can sit quietly and gently sway back and forth to achieve a similar trance.

2. Once you are in a trance, make sure you are still so that you will not alert or startle the animal.

3. Send your intention to the animal and ask its permission to join with its consciousness. Wait for a response. They may give you some physical response or it may be energetic. If you feel it is no, then you may try again with a different

animal. If it is yes, you may proceed.

4. Visualize your consciousness as either a small sphere of white light or a spark that resides in the center of your brain.

5. Take a breath and on the exhale, gently send your consciousness sphere or spark to the mind of the animal. Make sure you do this gently so not to make the animal frightened or uncomfortable.

6. Allow your consciousness to merge with the consciousness of the animal. Take all the time you need. Do not rush this process. Remember that this is a gentle process.

7. Simply observe. See through the eyes of the animal, hear through the animal's ears, feel the body of the animal, feel the emotions of the animal, and observe the animal's thoughts. You are not attempting to control the animal in any way. You are along for the ride in order to learn about the consciousness of the animal.

8. When you are ready to disengage from the animal's mind. Then, using your breath, inhale and as you do so bring back your consciousness to your mind.

9. Journal your observations.

Mental Shapeshifting

Mental shapeshifting is when we are changing shape with our minds through visualization. To change our shape into an animal we literally have to think like an animal. By doing all the previous shapeshifting exercises of research, observation, and joining our consciousness with an animal, we are learning how to think like that animal. This should not be too difficult for us because, as we learned at the beginning of this chapter, we already have animal consciousness within us in with the limbic system of the brain. Now we are going to focus on our own animal consciousness to tune into the consciousness of our animal. This is important because in order to do the next step of astral shapeshifting we must have a good understanding of how to shapeshift our minds.

1. For this technique, it will help if you are moving in order to reach a state of trance. You may choose either ecstatic dancing our shaking and swaying seidr.
2. Slow the dance or seidr down to a nice rhythmic pace making sure to stay in trance.
3. Focus on the limbic system of the brain. Remember, the center is the reptilian brain and the area just around it is the limbic system that is most akin to animal consciousness.
4. Take some nice deep breaths and focus on the mammalian brain. Place your everyday consciousness (the neocortex) aside and allow the animal mind of the limbic system to come through.
5. Now, mentally visualize yourself as this animal. Visualize the animal in every detail.
6. Enjoy this process. Once you are tuned into the animal mind you will start thinking, and perhaps moving like an animal. Allow this process to happen.
7. When you are ready, disengage your consciousness form the limbic system and bring back your everyday mind.
8. If you went especially deep with this technique, it would be a good idea to ground and center.
9. Journal your experience.

In some rare cases, some people may spontaneously go into etheric and physical shapeshifting. This is not a bad thing, if this happens, enjoy the experience, but make sure you remain in control. Even if you shapeshift into an animal you still have the human control of the neocortex should you need it. We still are responsible for our actions even in animal form.

Astral Shapeshifting

The next stage in shapeshifting is to shapeshift in the astral plane. While we are journeying, we will discover many wondrous worlds. There are many places of beauty and healing in the Otherworld, but there are also places of danger. While journeying you may need to shapeshift into your Spirit Animal or your animal helper. Shapeshifting into your Spirit Animal or animal helper can help you fend off or escape danger as well as take you to magical places very quickly. Sometimes, we may shapeshift into a bird in order to fly up to the Upperworld. Other times, we may shapeshift into a snake or mole to quickly journey down into the Underworld. When I was first learning how to explore the Midworld, I was taught to astrally shapeshift different animals so that I could explore from the point of view of that animal as well as travel at a much faster rate than just walking on my two legs. When I was exploring the deep forests of the Midworld I learned to shapeshift into a hare. By doing so, I was able to explore the nooks and crannies of the forest floor and meet many Otherworldly beings and animals. When I was exploring the skies, I shapeshifted into a bird. When I explored the oceans and rivers I shapeshifted into a fish. Yes, of course, when you are journeying you do not *have* to shapeshift into animals to explore these things, but it certainly has many advantages such as speed, animal instinct, strength, as well as the magick that each of those animals possesses. The major difference with mental shapeshifting and astral shapeshifting is that not only are we tapping into our animal consciousness, but we are accessing our astral body as well.

1. For this technique you can lie down and perform one of the astral journeying exercises. If you prefer to journey while using ecstatic dance or shaking and swaying seidr you certainly can. Try both ways and see which one resonates with you.

2. Once you are in a trance, visualize yourself going to the World Tree. You see the mighty branches of the tree stretching into the far reaches of the cosmos. When you look down, you see the ancient roots growing deeper and deeper into the center of the earth.

3. Decide if you would like to shapeshift into your Spirit Animal or one of your animal helpers.

4. Visualize yourself changing your shape into that of the animal. In the astral plane, it is easy to change your astral body into any shape you like. All you have to do is visualize and focus on your energies. See yourself as the animal in every detail. Visualize your animal body, your face, your limbs, and anything you can think of that is that animal.

5. Now, explore the Otherworld. If you have four legs, run as fast as you can and explore. If you are a bird, fly up into the skies and explore. If you are a fish, visualize an ocean or river and swim as fast as you can and explore.

6. If you like, you can shapeshift into another animal and continue exploring. Once you are finished, come back the way you came to the World Tree.

7. Change back into human form. Thank the Great Animal Spirit in which you changed into.

8. Journal your experience. Anything of interest you found in the Otherworld make sure you write it down so you can visit it again.

When you are journeying, you can shapeshift into anything you like. You are on the astral plane and you are only limited by your imagination and visualization. If you like, on full moons and sabbats, you may join witches in the astral for ritual and magick at the Witch's Sabbat. There are meeting places where witches shapeshift on the astral plane and then fly in animal form to dance and make magick. They are usually found on mountain tops, sea shores, valleys, and in deep forests. Some witches have the ability to hear the call of the Witch's God and fall into a trance and follow his music to the sabbat. Other witches follow their instinct and just "know" where the sabbath is. You can also ask your familiar or Spirit Animal to guide you to the Witch's Sabbat. Visualize yourself shapeshifting into your animal and follow your Spirit Animal to the Sabbat. There, you will honor the witch gods as well as meet other witches.

Etheric and Physical Shapeshifting

Etheric and physical shapeshifting is the changing of our etheric bodies and in extreme and rare cases the physical body. This is where we get the folklore of werewolves and other shape changers that are told in stories of myth and legends. When we shapeshift with our etheric bodies, we are changing the body that is closely related to the physical body. As we remember, the etheric body lies between the astral body and the physical body. When someone dies and the physical body is cast off, the spiritual, mental, astral, and etheric bodies remain. Sometimes, after some time after death, the etheric body is cast off, but it still contains some of the person's energy and likeness and can be seen by the living. This is one of the ways ghosts are seen after someone has died. One of the purposes of the etheric body is to help subtle energies (ch'i, prana, life force) process energies from the earth and the cosmos into the physical bodies. This is also the body where we find chakras and the Chinese meridian energy channels.

Once we become adept at shapeshifting mentally and astrally, we can further our experience by shapeshifting our etheric bodies. More often, this is the furthest we can go with shapeshifting. When we shapeshift our mental, astral, and etheric bodies, sometimes the energies are so strong that during the nighttime, especially under a full moon, some people perceive us as were-animals. To those who have psychic ability, we may look as though we have shapeshifted our physical body when in reality it is our etheric body. By shapeshifting etherically, we are able to harness the power of the animal directly into our physical bodies. When we do this, we are able to protect ourselves better, have more strength, stamina, and heal at a much faster rate. We also have the added benefit of being able to understand our Spirit Animal in a much deeper meaningful way. Many years ago, I was walking on a crosswalk when a car going 30 miles an hour did not see me and came barreling through. Through adrenaline, my animal instinct kicked in and rather than be thrown a few feet back and hurt myself, my Spirit Animal came through and I etherically shapeshifted. While shapeshifting, I placed my hands on the car's hood, balanced myself up until the car stopped. I then used the momentum of the stop to propel myself back and land on my feet. I looked at the driver and said, "Are you okay?" The driver lost all color in his face and asked me the same. "I'm fine, I said. "Have a good day!"

Because shapeshifting is a regular practice for me, when I was in danger and needed to shapeshift to protect myself, my instinct kicked in automatically. I did not need prompting or to even think of my shapeshifting techniques. It just happened because the limbic system; the animal consciousness, kicked in. When shapeshifting is a regular practice for you it can protect you from many things.

I want to take a moment and talk about control. I have seen many people practice shapeshifting and brag about losing control to the point of losing their rational human consciousness and harming other people or themselves. Yes, it is true that in order to etherically shapeshift you must let your rational human mind of the neocortex be placed aside so the animal brain of the limbic system can gain control. The key description here is "pushed aside", not "lost completely." A true witch or Spirit Walker adept has control over all techniques. Always. As a student you are learning these techniques and you are practicing so you may not have full control just yet. But it is what we strive for. Losing control during shapeshifting does not mean you are very powerful. It means you have not mastered the control you need to be a true adept. That is ok. That is what practice is for. We are all still learning the best we can.

I personally have never seen someone physically shapeshift all the way into animal form. I believe it is possible, but I have never seen it. Nor have I attempted to do so myself. The last thing I need is someone to go shooting at a Mountain Lion in the parks of Chicago. I think for a witch or Spirit Walker, it is perfectly fine to stop at etheric shapeshifting. This technique is powerful and has many magical benefits that can help us on our spiritual path. Are there people out there who can actually turn into a wolf, a bear, or a coyote? As we say in magick, anything is possible!

With this technique, you will be incorporating the previous exercises of mental and astral shape shifting as include etheric shapeshifting.

1. You may use the trance techniques of ecstatic dance or shaking and swaying seidr.

2. As you move into your trance, let the rational human mind be put aside. Tune in to the animal consciousness of the limbic system. I do this by visualizing the spark of my consciousness go to the center of my mind where the limbic system would be.

3. Spend some time shaking, swaying, and moving while focusing on the animal mind. Allow the consciousness of the animal within you to come out.

4. Keep moving, shaking and swaying. Go deeper and deeper. Know you have control over the whole experience. You know you can go as deep as you want to and still maintain control and come back to your rational human mind at any time.

5. Take deep breaths. Breath the life force energy from the earth into your body. This life force will give you power and magick to etherically shapeshift.

6. Feel your Spirit Animal within you wanting to come out. Your Spirit Animal is becoming more and more aggressive as it wants to come out and play and experience the physical world. You may begin making sounds your Spirit Animal would make.

7. Keeping shaking and swaying. Go deeper into the animal mind. Let it come out! Go deeper and deeper! Keep shaking and swaying! Let the animal out! Keep breathing!

8. Visualize your astral body take the shape of your Spirit Animal. Keep shaking and swaying!

9. You may begin to growl, howl, bark, yelp, or make other animal noises. This is great! Let it happen. Do not inhibit the process.

10. Feel your etheric body, the energy body between your astral and physical body, change into the shape of your Spirit Animal! Once your Spirit Animal is out and your mental, astral, and etheric bodies have shapeshifted, allow yourself to play. Run around the natural area you are in. If you are doing it with a group of people, interact with each other. Be mindful of being too aggressive with each other!

11. When you are ready, allow your rational mind to take full control and send the animal mind back to the center of your brain. Feel your etheric body returning to human form. Visualize your astral body changing back into human form.

12. Ground and center. Journal your experience.

Shapeshifting for Healing

Shapeshifting can be used to heal the physical body. When we etherically shapeshift, we are calling upon the powerful animal energies that lie deep in our animal minds in our limbic system. We are reaching deep into our consciousness to tap into our ability to heal our bodies. We have all heard about people who have the ability to heal much faster than the normal person. Scientists are discovering how the mind helps or detracts from the healing process of the physical body. When we are shapeshifting into our Spirit Animal, we are calling upon the magick of the limbic system and powers we are just beginning to understand. I cannot guarantee that you will have miraculous results each time you use shapeshifting to heal, but with regular practice and focus on the work at hand you should have good results. Speaking as a healer myself, healing is very individual. Not every technique and modality will work the same for every single person. This is why there are so many healing modalities out there and each have varying results depending upon the practitioner and the recipient. For myself, I have seen really good results.

1. Perform the etheric shapeshifting technique.
2. As you shake and sway, go deeper and deeper into the shapeshifting experience. Go deep into the animal consciousness.
3. Maintain communication with your Spirit Animal at the same time you are shifting.
4. Bring your attention to the animal healing powers that is inherent in all of us. Know that this power is universal in all life on earth.
5. As you continue to shake and sway and shapeshift, feel the healing energy of your Spirit Animal coming from your core and expanding out to your entire body. Remember, all animals have healing energy or what Native Americans call "medicine".
6. Feel the animal healing energy encompass your bones, your organs, your muscles, and your skin. Know that every cell is regenerating at a much faster rate.

7. When you are ready, thank your Spirit Animal and allow the animal healing energy to go back to your core and back into the animal consciousness.
8. Bring your shapeshifting to an end. Center and ground.
9. Journal your experience.

Shapeshifting For Protection

Shapeshifting can help you a great deal when you need to protect yourself from physical harm. Many times, those of us who regularly practice shapeshifting, when we are in danger, we automatically tap into our Spirit Animal and shapeshifting. This is because when we are angry, frightened, or threatened our sympathetic nervous system kicks in. This is when the blood runs from the center of the body to our extremities. Commonly, this is called our "fight or flight response". We either have to run away from the threat or stay and fight. When we are in danger, we do not have time to go over the entire etheric shapeshifting technique. We could be in trouble by then. What I have found that happens is that your animal instinct of self preservation kicks in and the Spirit Animal is *pulled* out of your deep mind and into your everyday waking consciousness. Yes, it is very much like Marvel's *The Incredible Hulk.* Essentially the "anger" or "fight or flight" automatically kicks in without so much of a thought.

There is a danger though. Sometimes when we shapeshift into our Spirit Animal for protection and engage in a fight or battle, we may go into a battle frenzy. The Berserkers would shapeshift into bears and go into a battle frenzy so that they would defeat their enemies. Our purposes with shapeshifting for protection is never to harm more than we have to protect ourselves. We do not want to cause serious harm or death to someone. Our goal is to stop them from hurting us or someone we love. When we shapeshift for protection you will call upon the strength, agility, and power of your Spirit Animal, but you will still maintain control. In order to do this technique successfully, you must practice shapeshifting regularly. Please make sure you use this technique as a last resort. If we are able, walking away and maintaining peace is always preferable. Also, we NEVER use shapeshifting to simply attack someone.

1. When you are in danger, focus your attention to the core of your body as well as the limbic system (animal mind).
2. Allow yourself to call upon your pure animal instinct of survival. Allow yourself to become angry and territorial.
3. Quickly, pull your Spirit Animal from your animal mind and bring it about into your physical being.
4. Allow your Spirit Animal to take over your body just enough so that you are still in control.
5. Know that you have more strength than you once had. Know that you are faster than you once were. Know that you have more agility than you once did.
6. When the threat is over, return your Spirit Animal to your deep mind.
7. Center and ground.

Chapter 7

Nature Spirits

Everything in nature is alive. All trees, plants, stones, and waterways are alive and have an in-dwelling spirit. When we walk through a wooded area we can sometimes feel like the trees and vegetation are watching us. As the winds blow through the branches of trees it may seem as though they are singing the songs of the deep wood and the connection of all things. As we journey deeper into the forest, we are entering the home of the spirits of nature. Nature Spirits are connected to the earth's life force. They have the magical ability to bring the energies of earth to us and help them manifest on the surface. It is because of this magical process that all life is able to thrive and roam the earth.

Nature Spirits want to work with humans and animals. They are synergistic with us. Plants give us oxygen and we give them carbon dioxide. We eat plants to live and when humans and animals die, our decaying flesh give them nutrients to flourish. They also have the power to bring balance and healing into our lives. Many plants can give us medicine to heal or bodies, but they can also give us medicine to heal our energies and our emotions. We are connected with Nature Spirits and they are connected with us. It was not until the last hundred years or so that many people have lost their connection to nature. We live in cities and suburbs that, many times, have very little plant life. Because of this, we are cut off from their healing power. I firmly believe that this is one of the reasons that more and more people are having high anxiety and having more diseases than we used to. We need to reconnect with Nature Spirits so that we may find wholeness and balance with nature and the Universe.

Any time you are having a stressful time in your life go out into nature. Take a walk and breathe in the energies of the trees and plants around you. Smell the fragrance of flowers and listen to the movement of trees and bushes in the wind. Just as plants take our carbon dioxide and give us oxygen, they also take our energies of stress and give us healing and relaxing energies. This is another way that we are synergistic with plants. I have a quick little exercise for you. Go outside to any tree. Place your hands upon the bark of the tree and connect to the physical tree for a moment. Take a breath and send your stress and anxiety down through your feet and into the roots of the tree. Now, breathe in the relaxing and healing energies from the tree into your hands and into your body. Continue this cycle for a few breaths. Breathe in healing energy from the trunk and exhale your stress into the roots. Both you and the tree are receiving energies that you need. Give the tree your heartfelt thanks when you are finished.

When I was first learning Native American spirituality, one of the first things that my teacher, Billie Topa Tate, said to me was that I needed to make sure I have plants in my life. I should not only eat more plants, but I needed to make sure that there were plants in my home and in my spiritual practice. A healer should always have plants around. They will teach us many things about the earth, healing, and our connection to the Web of Wyrd. Nature Spirits want to help us. They have a fondness for humans. They want to see us succeed and be happy. They want us to be whole. In order for us to learn their healing gifts we must first establish a relationship with Nature Spirits.

While the physical part of the plant can help heal our bodies, the Nature Spirits can help heal our energy bodies and spirit. Many times, the imbalances that cause us illness have an emotional or spiritual cause. Universal energies are constantly at play to bring us into situations that are designed to teach us how to spiritually grow and evolve. When illness happens to us, we are given an opportunity from the Universe to learn from our mistakes and transform our negative emotions such as fear, anger, worry, and so forth, into energies that bring us gratitude, happiness, and love. Nature Spirits understand that we are only human and that we may need help finding healing from time to time. Nature Spirits enjoy helping humans transcend beyond the pain and suffering of illness and seek to bring us back into harmony with the Earth and the Universe as a whole. They are able to do this by helping us heal our spiritual and emotional wounds.

I teach my students that we should never judge a person upon their path of healing. We really do not know where someone has been before they got to our healing space. What may seem easy to us may be very difficult for them. We do not know how someone grew up or even cultural differences. We do not know about the things that affected them growing up and how they handle stressful situations. Everyone is different and everyone has a different way they handle life circumstances. It is not for us to judge them. It is for us to help them find balance within themselves. Even if you do not heal the public and you are only learning about Nature Spirits for your own healing, try not to judge yourself for past mistakes and how we respond to things. When it comes to self-healing, do the best you can to become a better person, have gratitude for what the Universe has done for you and take things one step at a time.

Nature Spirits have compassion for us. As I said before, humans and nature are designed to live in harmony with each other. They seek to heal us and we should seek to heal them when they need us. Nature Spirits are just that; spirits. They have the ability to transcend time and space and go within our energy and spiritual bodies and find the core of the disharmony and pain. They can weave a spiritual web that patches up our spiritual wound and brings us healing. Well, what does that look like? When Nature Spirits heal us, they create an energetic/ spiritual signature in our bodies that attract learning and healing situations. Sometimes memories come flooding back about situations that you may still need to deal with. Sometimes an opportunity comes up that you may need to forgive someone for a past action against you. Or perhaps a realization comes to you that you did no wrong and you are doing the best you can with the situation at hand. Everyone's healing is different and these are only a couple of the many situations that could possibly occur. Keep in mind, when we ask Nature Spirits to help us heal, we are asking them to go to the core of our energies and our spirits for true healing, not just a temporary fix.

It is important to establish a relationship with Nature Spirits. Just as with a human being, we have to have a relationship with Nature Spirits so that we many learn to understand them, not only intellectually, but also on a level of spirit. This is where true understanding lies. By connecting to them on a spiritual level, we will be able to understand their purpose and their powers of healing. We will also learn to have more compassion for them. I have found that many plants want to befriend us and yet we do not friend them back. By strengthening the bond with Nature Spirits our own well-being and connection to nature with also be strengthened.

Observation of Nature

The first thing you must do in order to start a relationship with Nature Spirits is to go out into nature and just observe. Ideally, you will want to go out into a part of nature that is far away from people as possible. For those of us who live in cities it may be a bit more difficult. If you are able, find a park or a nature preserve so that you may be able to do your work with Nature Spirits. It is also beneficial to take a day trip to a place in nature that is undisturbed by humans. However, you can still work with Nature Spirits in your own backyard, garden, or even potted plants. The important thing is that you begin establishing a relationship with these magical beings.

Paracelsus was a Swiss physician during the Renaissance who

studied astrology and alchemy. He came up with the idea of *The Doctrine Of Signatures* which states that God placed a signature on all plants that tell the herbalist what the plant was meant for. For example, any flower or plant that was shaped like the liver would help heal the liver. It also says that the color of the plant told you how it can be used. Any plant that has red petals, leaves, or fruit can help with blood pathologies. Likewise, any plant that seem to ooze a mucus like substance could be used to heal colds and infections. This is an excellent thought to keep in mind as we are observing things in nature. If you are observing a flower, what color is its petals? How tall does it grow? What shape does the flower look like? Similar observances can be used for semi-precious stones. Typically, we can tell by the color of a stone what chakra it is good for. Clear quartz is good for crown chakra, purple stones for the brow, blue stones for the throat, green or pink for the heart, gold or yellow for solar plexus, orange for navel, and red for root chakras. When we are observing trees you can ask yourself; How tall does it grow? What do the leaves look like? Does the tree flower in the spring? Is the tree an evergreen or do its leaves fall in autumn? In the book *Plant Spirit Shamanism: Traditional Techniques for Healing the Soul,* Ross Heaven and Howard G. Charing state, "Shamans distinguish the spiritual powers and qualities of the plants in many ways: by the color of their flowers, their perfumes, the shape of their leaves, where they are growing and in what ways, the mood they evoke…"

Another thing to keep in mind when we are observing plants in nature is what type of climate does it like? Does it like prairies or cliffs? Does it like lots of light or does it prefer dim light? Arnica is a plant that is used to treat broken bones and wounds. Interestingly, arnica grows near mountains. I suppose the arnica spirits thought it wise to grow near a mountain in case anyone should fall! As for stones, where are they formed, and the substances they are formed from, may be of special importance.

Obsidian stones are black and they are formed from the cooling of lava. Therefore, obsidian stones are considered fiery in nature and are often used in earth magick as well as scrying for spirits. Pink Calcite is a pink stone that is brittle in nature. Therefore, pink calcite is a wonderful stone to use to heal the brittleness of a broken heart.

Observing different types of water can tell you many things about the nature of water spirits. A slow moving and gentle stream can reveal a water spirit that is gentle and cleansing to the spirit. A rushing river can give you hints about the power that the river spirits commands. One of my favorite places to go in the United States is the mountains in Palm Springs, California. There is a legend about an evil shaman named Tahquitz. Tahquitz became very powerful and he began to harm the people and steal away beautiful young women. The chief of the tribe had to banish the shaman away to the canyon in the mountains to save his people. The chief, Algoot, battled the evil Tahquitz and eventually the shaman was defeated. But the shaman did not die. He turned himself into a 50-foot waterfall that continues to pour down the canyon till this day. They say that you must be careful of picking beautiful flowers to smell them. For, the evil Tahquitz was using his magick to charm you into a trance to spirit you away deep into the mountain. Before I heard this story, I knew the waterfall in the canyon was a shaman or magician of some kind. I felt his mighty power and how he watched over the canyon. By observing this natural phenomenon, I was able to detect the magick of the waterfall.

Working With Nature

To the witch or Spirit Walker, relationships are important to maintain balance and healing. I cannot say this enough and it bears repeating. If you are working with plant medicines, trees, stones, water ways, or any other part of nature, it is vital that you have a connection with the spirit. The first things you will need to do when working with Nature Spirits is to work with the Spirit of Place. The Spirit of Place is the spirit that watches over and governs the natural environment. When I want to work a ceremony or work with the spirits in an area of nature I will connect with the Spirit of Place and ask their permission to do my magick. If I neglect to do this sometimes I will get a feeling that I am forgetting something. This is when it pops into my head, "Oops! How rude! I forgot to ask the Spirit of place if I can work here!" Then I explain to the guardian spirit my purpose for my magick that day and give a small offering.

There are times when the Spirit of Place will say "no". When this happens, albeit rare, I respect the spirit's wishes and find another place in nature to work. There may be higher spiritual forces at work that I do not need to disturb. Also, sometimes the spirit just does not want to be bothered. Either way, always respect the wishes of the spirits. Many times, when I ask the Spirit of Place if I may work in their area, they will not say anything directly to me, but instead, will give me a feeling. If it is a "yes" then the feeling is welcoming. If "no" then it feels like I am not supposed to be there. When you get the permission of the Spirit of Place your magick will be more powerful and often times, the spirit will aid you in your magick.

Developing Relationships

The first thing you will need to do when developing relationships with Nature Spirits is to journey to them in the Otherworld. This is a fantastic exercise because this allows you to get to know the Nature Spirit on a personal level. Observation and research are very helpful, but having a one on one relationship will give you insight into the spirit and the plant, stone, or water that no one else can. When I am journeying out in nature, I usually like to use a rattle as my "drum beat". It is small and can easily fit in a bag that I can carry around with me. But if you feel more spiritual using a drum then do it! However, journeying will be the best approach.

1. Go out in nature and decide what Nature Spirit you want to establish a relationship with. It can be a plant, tree, stone, river, lake, etc.
2. State your intention to the Spirit of Place. Leave an offering as thanks to the spirit. If the Spirit of Place says "no" then find another place in nature and ask again.
3. Begin using your drum or rattle go into a light trance. It is ok not to use a beat if you enjoy journeying without one.
4. With this technique, you are not going anywhere but where you are, only in the Otherworld. Once you have established a trance, open your heart chakra and send energy to the plant, stone, tree, or water. Explain your intention to get to know the spirit and establish a relationship with them.
5. The spirit may show itself in many ways. For myself, they often appear as human like beings that I can easily communicate with. Sometimes they appear as the plant or stone, but with human like features such as eyes, ears, nose, and mouth. This is where we get the idea of The Green Man from. He is the nature spirit of the green wood. However, nature spirits will appear to you in whatever way is easier for you to understand.
6. Introduce yourself just as you would to a human being. Tell them your name and ask for theirs. Spend some time getting to know them. Once you have done that, then you can ask them about their magical qualities and healing abilities.
7. Ask the permission of the spirit if it is alright to take a little of the plant so that you may work with the spirit further.
8. Once you are done speaking with the spirit, say your goodbyes and leave an offering.

9. Journal your experience.

Offerings to Nature Spirits

We should always give offerings to Nature Spirits when we are working with them. The best offerings that I have found are water, tobacco, and your own personal energy. All life on earth needs water to survive. It is also a great conduit for energy and intention. We can place our intention and energy into a bit of water and poor it into the roots of the plant or place water on top of a stone. Here in the United States, I have found that the spirits enjoy good pipe tobacco. Good tobacco is sweet smelling and carries a nice charge of energy. Nature Spirits love it! I will often place a pinch of tobacco as an offering to the spirits when I work with them. You can also easily use your own personal energy as an offering. There have been times when I had no tobacco or water on me and I wanted to leave an offering to the Nature Spirits. Remember, animals and plants have a synergistic relationship so they love our energy as well. When I want to leave an offering of energy I will either touch the plant or stone or hold my hand over it and send my energy through my hands and into the plant, stone, or water.

Dreaming

We can learn many things about the powers of plants, trees, and stones by dreaming with them. To many witches and Spirit Walkers, there is no difference between the dreamworld and the Otherworld; they are one and the same. When we dream, our spirits fly to the Otherworld. There is no past, present, or future. There is only the presence of being. The true form of Nature Spirits lives in this world and this is one of the best ways to communicate with them and learn their wisdom. Dreaming with plants, trees, and stones is a wonderful way to learn about the powers and magick of Nature Spirits.

1. You may pick an herb, plant, stone, or a small stick from a tree to dream with. Make sure to leave the spirit an offering at the site where you found them.
2. Before bed, spend some time holding the object in your hand and talk to the Nature Spirit. Tell them that you would like them to visit you in your dreams so that you can learn from their wisdom and healing abilities.
3. Leave a small offering of tobacco or water for the spirit.
4. Place the object in a small pouch or bag and put under your pillow.
5. State your intention to the spirits to dream with the Nature Spirit.
6. As you drift off to sleep say prayers to The Creator and the Nature Spirit so that you will learn of their wisdom in your dreams.
7. When you awaken, journal your dream experience. If you do not remember your dreams, that's ok! Journal how you felt during the night. Journal any emotions or impressions you feel when you wake up. The dreams will come with practice.

Many times, the dreams you will have will not be the plant or stone coming to you in your dream, but rather the spirit will give you a dream of what its powers are. For example, when I was first learning to dream with sage, I would have dreams of purification and being in a place of happiness and balance. As we know, sage is good for ridding your space of negative energy. Try not to judge the dream itself. The important thing is what the dream is trying to show you.

Sacred Nature Songs

Each plant, tree, and stone have a sacred song. The more you meditate and journey with the nature object, the more things that it will teach you. One of those things is a sacred song. In my training with my Native American teachers, they have taught me to listen with my heart for a song. The song does not have to make any sense to anyone else but you! This is a song that you will sing when you are planning to ask the help of the Nature Spirit in healing sessions, be it your own or one you are facilitating for someone else. When the Nature Spirit gives you a song it may have words or just vocables. These songs may just have sounds like "fa la la la" or "hey hey hey" or "ah ah ah". Many of the Lakota traditional songs I have been given by my teachers or the Nature Spirits are mainly vocables. It is not the sounds that come out but the intention behind the sounds that makes something a sacred song.

Listening to the Song of Nature

1. Use a recording device to record the songs the spirits give you. When you begin this exercise make sure you are recording.

2. Journey with the nature object just as in previous exercises.

3. Ask the spirit to give you a song you may call them by so they can help you with healing.

4. With your heart, listen carefully for a song. You may "hear" the song in your mind or you may be inspired to sing words or vocables. Either way is fine. Do not try to edit the song. Let it come out naturally.

5. When you hear the song, sing or hum it out loud so it may be recorded by your device.

6. If you are having a hard time "hearing" the song, keep humming or singing anything that you are able to hear. If you have not heard the whole song, end the exercise and try again the next day. Most songs are simple and are about one to five minutes long. Many times, you will just hear one verse that you are to repeat four times. One time per direction for east, south, west, and north.

If you do not hear anything you can try creating a song based on the feeling that the plant or nature object is giving you. Focus on the feeling you are getting from the object and begin humming or singing vocables. Keep practicing with the object everyday so that eventually a song comes forth. You can use this song to call the nature spirit to come into your ceremonies and healing practice.

Healing Uses of Nature Spirits

There are several ways you can ask Nature Spirits to aide you in the healing process. We can ingest the plant, use the smoke, or place them in a medicine bag. When using the Nature Spirits of stones and most trees, it is better to place them somewhere on the body. In this case of stones, I like to place certain stones and crystals on the major chakra points. Please remember, before ingesting any plant make sure you do some research on it to make sure it is not toxic. A quick internet search can tell you right away. Any herb you can find at your local health food store in the form of tea should be fine. If you do not know what a plant is do not ingest it. In this case, you can work with the Nature Spirit for energy healing, but do so only with the spirit of nature. Before you use Nature Spirits for healing, make sure you do all the above exercises to you can have a relationship with the spirit and it can understand what needs to be healed.

Herbal Teas

One of the best ways to work with the spirit of a plant is through the use of a tea. You can get many organic herbs from herb stores or health food stores. Again, before ingesting anything you will need to do some basic research to make sure it is not toxic. You can make teas two ways: an infusion or decoction. An infusion is when we pour boiling water on flowers and leaves and some stems. The plant is thinner here and it only takes a few minutes. Before pouring the water on your herb make sure you tell the spirit what you are asking it to heal. A decoction is when you boil the plant. Roots and hard stems needed to be boiled for a few minutes in water because of their thickness. How do you know when you are done? For me, I look at the color of the water. When it has the color that you like then you are done. Try not to over boil though. After boiling you can take the used plants out with a strainer.

Smoke

The smoke from plants are a wonderful way to use the powers of the Nature Spirits. Pagans often give the spirits and gods offerings of incense because the smoke of the plant or resin wisps up into the air and seems to disappear into the spirit world. I was taught by Native American spiritual leaders that when you are using an herb such as sage, tobacco, cedar, or sweet grass the first thing you do is pray to the spirit of the plant and tell it what is wrong with the affected person. You also pray to Creator asking them to help the person to heal. Then you use a fan or feather and fan the smoke over the person and the affected area. When I do this, I will visualize the spirit of the plant going into the person's energy bodies to help in the healing process. I will then give the spirit an offering of tobacco as thanks.

Medicine bag

The medicine bag is one of my favorite ways to incorporate the healing powers of Nature Spirits. I will place things like herbs, stones, bones, fur, leaves, or any other natural object into a small pouch that I can hang around my neck or place in my pocket. This is a great way to have the spirit of these things work on your spirit for healing. By placing natural objects in a medicine bag, you are asking the Nature Spirit of each item to help heal your energy bodies. This is a valuable healing technique because, as we talked about earlier, the Nature Spirit can work on the emotional, mental, and spiritual cause of the illness and help you find balance and health. You can also place herbs that are not necessarily good to ingest in your medicine bag because it is only going to work on your spirit. Again, pray to the Nature Spirit and ask them to help you in healing. The Nature Spirits will gladly do so. Do not forget to give them an offering.

Meeting Mother Earth

The greatest of all Nature Spirits is our Mother Earth. As witches and Spirit Walkers, we know that Mother Earth is not a symbol or just a scientific model. She is a living being. She is a great and mighty goddess. In Greco-Roman mythology, Mother Earth, named Gaia, was the mother of all the gods. She was formed out of chaos and created an equal for herself, Ouranos, the sky. She is the mother of all things. We have the ability to meet with our primordial mother. We can have a relationship with her. We should have a relationship with her! If everyone learned to care for our Mother Earth then there would be no pollution and humanity would be happier and healthier. We should visit with the goddess and ask her what she needs from us. We should give her ceremonies, healing energy, and resources so that we can aide in her healing process. After all, she is our Mother.

Journey To Mother Earth

1. This exercise can be done inside but it is better to be out in a place of nature. Sit on the ground. You may use a chair if that is better suited for you.
2. Spend some time observing nature. Observe the animals, insects, and birds doing their daily routine. Feel the sun on your face and listen for the wind to blow around you.
3. Feel the earth beneath you. Focus on your aura and expand it outward to feel the pulse of the earth and life itself. All of this is Mother Earth.
4. Close your eyes and relax your body. Take deep breaths and bring yourself into a light trance state.

5. Send your astral body down into the depths of the earth. Have the intention of going to where Mother Earth lives.

6. Allow her to appear before you as she will. Spend some time speaking with her and getting to know her on a deeper levelAsk her what she needs of you and how you can help heal her.

7. When you are ready, bring your consciousness back to your body.

8. Leave an offering for her. You may leave food that the animals can eat. You may also leave an offering of your personal energy for her healing.

9. Journal you experience.

Chapter 8

Elves and Faeries

One cannot help but to associate Elves and Faeries to the world of magick. It is sometimes said that they literally *are* magick. The Elves and Faeries are a part of nature. They live in harmony with the energies and vibrations of the earth. They are synergistic to the cycles of life, death, the rebirth of the land. Elves and Faeries live very closely to the land so it is not difficult to see how people believe them to be made of the substance of magick. Elves and Faeries are very similar to each other in form and their powers of magick. From my experience and research with both these races, I have found that there are more similarities than differences. So, it appears that the major difference is only in geographical location and lore. Faeries are generally located in Celtic countries while the Elves are found in Nordic or Germanic speaking countries. They speak the language of the country that they are found in as well as their own native tongue. Elves and Faeries both have a love of dancing and music while having a disdain for iron and steel objects. They both have great healing power as well as the power of glamour and trickery. The most important similarity is that they are both connected to the land in heart and spirit.

One of the few things that they seem to differ on is human interaction. Throughout the myths and lore, Faeries do not like human beings very much and it takes a lot to gain their trust. We cannot blame them for this. While it is part of the Faery and Elf way to heal and protect the Mother Earth, many humans have committed themselves to the destruction of the earth's resources. We constantly destroy forests, over mine the earth, and pollute the oceans and air. They also have observed many humans who lack honor and integrity. Faeries are known for having a disdain for anyone who lacks honor and hospitality. If we cannot show kindness to each other, how are we then to show kindness to the Faeries? Elves, on the other hand, seem to be more patient with us humans. In the lore of both Elves and Faeries, there have been many instances where a human has stumbled upon the Otherworld or they were taken. When they return, time has passed many years and even hundreds of years and the poor soul no longer recognizes anyone or anything of their home land. In his book *Elves, Wights, and Trolls,* Kveldulf Gundarsson says, "Some of the characteristics and dangers of the *sidhe* and alfs may be the same, but in general, the alfs are much better-disposed towards humankind, and likelier to ask, as well as offer, favour to those of whom they meet."

Elves

The Elves are known as the *alfar* or *alfs* in Germanic speaking countries. The word *alf* may mean "bright". When the elves are seen they appear to be very fair and bright. They seem to shine with an aura of brightness and beauty. The word *alf* may also mean "mists". Elves rarely take physical form in our world. When the elves allow us to see them, they may appear as mists taking human like form. They may have come to be called the *alfar* because when we see them with psychic focus, they often appear as beings of light or fog. During the middle ages, any being of nature was called an elf or alf. Before that time, elves were known to be very tall and mighty. I have heard a few different reasons for this. One of the reasons is because the people of the middle ages did not have the same understanding of the Mighty and Shining beings as the pagans did before Christianity came to the Germanic countries. They may have come to believe the term "alf" could be any spirit of nature. The second reason I have heard is that it was a way for Christian folk to negate the power of the Elves. They seemed more manageable if they were small woodland sprites who occasionally caused mischief. Before the middle ages, this was unheard of. I prefer to take the traditional meaning of the Elves that they are a mighty people who live in the Otherworld, while the woodland sprites and nature spirits are a different type of spirit all together. I have heard some people refer to them as the angels of the Nordic people. Angels are a completely different entity than the Elves. Both beings may be bright and have a distrust of humans, but Angels have a celestial energy about them while elves have the energy of nature. We must remember to treat every entity we encounter and work with as separate being.

There are two main types of Elves. There are the Light Elves and The Dark Elves. The Light Elves are bright and fair and live in Light Elf Home called Ljusalfheim. They are known for their powerful magick of healing. They live in harmony with all of nature and have a deep understanding on birth, life, and death. They are great smiths and have many magical weapons. They also seem to be welcoming to humans. I have found in my personal experience that the Light Elves have a fondness for those of us who are followers of earth-based spirituality. The Light Elves can be welcoming to us, but we still must earn their trust. They respond to common courtesy and politeness. If we make a deal with them, you must think long on hard on the agreement because once you break a deal with the elves it is very difficult to almost impossible to gain their trust back. The Light Elves will honor their word and they expect you to do this same. The Light Elves are often invited into the Heathen home during festival times. During the festival of Winter Nights, which takes place at the end of October, sometimes the alfs where honored with an *alfablot*, this was the honoring of the elves through the drinking horn. Once you make an ally with the Light Elves you have a powerful and magical friend who you can help you when needed and teach you much powerful magick. But remember, the Light elves will not simply give you their elvish secrets, just as with any magical teacher, you must earn the right to go deep into the magick of the wood and the deepest parts of nature.

The Dark Elves are somewhat different than the Light Elves but are essentially the same race. The Dark Elves live in the regions of the Underworld known as Svartalheim. This translates to "land of the dark elves". In his book, *The Pathwalkers Guide To The Nine Worlds,* Raven Kaldera says:

"Svartalheim is a dual land, divided above and below by the two races that live there-the Duergar (dwarves), who claim primary ownership of the world, but who chose instead to live underground in mountain caverns; and the Dark Alfar, who are immigrants and live partially above the earth and partially under it."

Throughout the lore related to the Dark Elves there seems to be different ideas of what the Dark Elves are. In some of the lore it is said the Dark Elves are the dwarves that live in the subterranean worlds below the earth. These are the beings who are short and stocky in stature and mine the caverns of the deep earth. They are the best blacksmiths in the Universe and have made such powerful tools as Thor's hammer and Odin's spear. They also make many things of beauty. They made the beautiful necklace that is worn by the goddess of love, Freya. They dwarves are hard bargainers and are weary of beings who try to take advantage of them. It seems to me that because the Dark Elves and Dwarves live in the same world, they may have gotten confused in the lore. Remember, to some, the world "alf" simply means "spirit" so to them the dwarves and Dark Elves are the same race.

There are other pieces of lore that say the Dark Elves live in the earth mounds throughout Europe. Because of this, they are associated with the ancestors and the mighty dead. In Celtic and Nordic countries there seems to be a little confusion, or disagreement, about the magick of the earth mounds and the residents. Some say that the mounds are a portal to the Alfland or Faeryland, while others say it is a portal to the Underworld and the land of the dead. It seems that this lore has become so confused that the stories and legends of the mounds have blended into each other. Many of the stories I have found say that the beings in the mounds are not actually Faeries or Elves but are the home of the dead. I have even seen legends that say that the mounds contain Faeries, Elves, *and* the ancestors. I can see why people get confused with some much conflicting lore. I have spent a lot of time researching the Underworld and the ancestors. In my research and experience, I have found that the mounds are portals to the Otherworld and the Underworld depending upon your desire of destination. Meaning, if you use the mound as a means of journeying you can decide if you want to go to the land of the elves or the land of the ancestors. Where you choose to travel in the Otherworld is entirely up to you.

According the elvish lore of the middle ages, not all elves were hospitable to humans. There are many stories about *elf shot*. Elf shot is said to be the stinging or stabbing pain that is suddenly felt while in the green wood. When this pain was felt, it was believed that the Elves had shot you with one of their elvish arrows. The magick from elf shot could cause many types of illnesses. It could be as mild as a jolting pain or as severe as causing swelling in the affected area, wasting away, or death. There were many charms to prevent and to treat elf shot. Later in the chapter we will talk about how to treat elfshot. Usually, the Elves do not attack unless they feel threatened in some way. They have the ability to see whom among us are caretakers of the earth, so therefore, they will usually not harm witches and Spirit Walkers such as us. As long as we treat them with courtesy and respect, we may tread into their lands peacefully.

Faeries

The Faeries are sometimes known as the *Sidhe* in Celtic countries.

They are a powerful and magical race and are similar to the Elves. They are tall shining and bright beings that glow with an aura of magick. The word "Faerie" comes from the French word "fey" which roughly translates to "magick". There are several theories of where the Faeries first originated. There is a theory that they were the Pygmy people who were the first residents of the Celtic countries and they were driven into the forests by invaders to become the Faeries. Some say that they are a race of gods known as the Tuatha De Danann which roughly translates to "the people of the Goddess Danu". The goddess Danu has been found to be from Denmark which lies just above Germany. Legends state that these people invaded Ireland and were later defeated themselves by a people known as The Sons of Mil. The Tuatha De Danann used their magick and crossed over into the Otherworld forever to be the race of the Faeries. I find it to be very interesting that the people of the goddess Danu were perhaps a race that came over from Germanic countries. Is this the reason that the Elves and Faeries are similar? Did some of the Elves migrate to the Celtic countries? I have worked with the Faeries for many years and I am led to believe that these magical beings are not some long-forgotten race of gods, but rather, beings who evolved as a part of nature. Faeries, like, Elves are one with nature. As we humans evolved into physical flesh, perhaps they evolved to live in a deeply synergistic ebb and flow of energy of the earth itself. But this is only my conjecture.

The Faeries have often been portrayed as little winged figures who dance in moonlit circles and grant wishes. Granted, they do love to dance and sing, but they are not the wood sprites that Victorian story tellers have made them out to be. The "little people" that are often called faeries are not the faeries that are spoken of in Celtic pagan lore. These beings are certainly real but are more akin to nature spirits. This is very much like when during the middle ages, after the coming of Christianity, that the word "elf" meant any spirit especially a nature spirit. So, during this same time, in Celtic countries, any being of nature was called a faerie. There are, however, many beings that are close to nature that one may stumble upon that are not necessarily Faeries. I think we do a disservice to the Faery race by portraying them as little winged figures. This became more common place in the Victorian period. At this time, the lore and stories were no longer being used to teach about the magick of the Fey. They were being diminished in size and power to show that magical creatures no longer had the power of the land they once did and that the ruling Christian Church had dominion throughout the land. I read in a book of Faeries once that said church bells banished faeries away. When I asked the Fey what they thought about the sound of church bells, they said they found them quite lovely.

Faeries are said to both live and have control over nature. They can live within trees, stones, rocks, and many other things. These objects of nature are not necessarily where faeries live, but are a portal into the Otherworld. They have the power to make the crops grow or to blight them. It would do you great benefit that if you are growing anything outside you should give the Faeries offerings of milk, honey, bread, or coins. Once an offering is given to the faeries, or any spirit for that matter, it should be left out in nature to decompose. The spirits will take the life force of the offering and the earth will take the physical shell back into her. They are guardians of nature, especially far off and secluded place in nature that do not see the frequent human visitors. Faeries do not trust humans and they often keep to themselves. It is very difficult to earn the trust of the faeries, even harder than earning the trust of the elves.

Their magick is very powerful. Witches have been seeking the aid of the Faeries for hundreds of years. Magick comes from nature and Faeries are a part of nature. They have a connection to the life force of the Universe that many humans will never have. They have great skill in the healing magical arts. Many witches have called upon faery magick to heal the sick in their time of need. They are also known for glamour. This is the ability to appear as any shape or form they wish, but it is only an illusion. They do, however, have the power to shapeshift and appear to be almost anything they want to be. Are they really shapeshifting or is faery magick that gives the illusion of shapeshifting? This is part of the wonder of the Fey. You are never quite sure what magick they are doing. They often appear as birds, rabbits, raccoons, and many other animals. Like elves, they may also appear as beings of light, mist, or fog. When you have established a relationship with the Fey, you will be able to recognize their energy and behavior patterns more easily.

The Fey are closely related to the life force energies of the earth. Essentially, they are caretakers of the natural Otherworld just as we should be caretakers of the physical world. Faeries have the ability to harness the earth energies for the benefit of the land and its inhabitants. Because the Fey live in the Otherworld, they have a better perspective of the ebb and flow of the energies that lie beneath the earth as well as on her surface. They have the ability to guide this energy that is beneficial to the health of the land. This is very similar to Feng Shui. When the earth energies are flowing without impediments, the health and vitality of the land is very strong. When the energies are low and full of blockages, the health withers and there is a feeling bad energy around. I believe this is what is meant when the folklore says the Fey give good or bad luck depending upon how they are treated. They can either strengthen or weaken the flow of the earth force.

Similarly to the Elves, there seems to be some confusion between the Faerie race and the dead. There are several accounts in traditional lore that speak of eye witness accounts of seeing the dead in the faery mounds and in the Otherworld. It is important to understand that the Faeries and the ancestors are not the same entities. So, how is it that people have seen the dead in the world of the Fey? One reason is that Fairies and Elves are infamous for "stealing" humans and taking them to the

Otherworld. They may have simply seen someone in the world of Faery who they presumed to be dead. Another reason is that I have found that upon death, humans have the choice of where they want to spend their afterlife. The dead may have wanted to join the Faeries upon death.

Faeries may be contacted at any time of the year but there are a few magical days that the veil between the worlds is thin and the world of the Fey and the physical world intermingle very easily. Beltaine is perhaps the most powerful day for contact with the Faeries. This is the first day of Celtic Summer. This is when the fires of the winter are extinguished and the new fires of summer lighted to welcome the warmth of the sun. This is the time when the land is alive and blooming with green and the colors of many flowers. The earth energies are flowing forth and the powers of the Faeries can be strongly felt. The time of Midsummer, or the pagan Litha, is also a powerful day. This is the point in the year of the longest day and marks the height of the season of growth. There are many tales of the Fey being seen and performing magick on this day. The most famous story is Shakespeare's *A Midsummer's Night Dream*. Samhain, often celebrated on November 1 is another time that the veil between the worlds is thin. This is the time of year when the energies of the earth are withdrawing from the land and the world seems to be dying. At this time, it is neither summer or winter and the energies are chaotic and have a darker tone. The dead come through into the world of living and sometimes the Faeries can be found among them. Samhain is a time of great transition with the land and Fey are tied to the energies of the land, so therefore they celebrate the time of decay as well.

During the time of Beltane and Samhain are usual times of the Faery procession. This is when the Fey are said to move their homes. They can sometimes be seen as balls of lights in the dark forest moving upon a faery road or spirit path. It is said that it is unwise to spy upon the Faeries as they process. They do not like to be spied upon and think it is very rude to do so. In fact, it will be very helpful to find someone who is well versed in Faery roads in processions because to build upon a faery road is to invite bad energies into your home or establishment. Think about how you feel when there is construction on the road you take to work and you have to take a detour.

I think it is very important for magical people to give offerings to the Faeries and Elves. When we give offerings, we are not only gaining their trust and favor, we are sharing our energies with them. They in return may grant us gifts of magick, luck, herbal wisdom and healing. There are a variety of offerings you can give the Faeries and the Elves. They are very fond of bread, honey, and milk. You may also pour out whiskey, wine, or mead directly on the ground as an offering to them. Elves and Faeries eat meat as well. They enjoy fish, pork, beef and venison. When we leave offerings in the woods or on a sacred shrine for the Elves and the Fey it is a good sign when an animal eats the food that is left. They may have shapeshifted into an animal to enjoy the food or they are possessing the animal and absorbing the energy of the offerings through them.

Many people who work with Elves and Faeries have discovered that they are not just restricted to their homeland of Germanic and Celtic countries. They are also in many different parts of the world. Some say that they traveled over to America and other countries when settlers arrived. Others say that there are Fairies and Elves that live naturally in all areas of the world. In our magical work, I do not think it matters if they traveled over to other countries or if they were the original inhabitants of that land. The important thing is to establish a relationship with them for the betterment of our spirituality and the magick of the environment in which we live.

Elf and Faery Magick
As witches and Spirit Walkers, it is important to maintain good

relationships with all beings in the Otherworld. We are all part of the Web of Wyrd and for better or worse and we have an effect on each other and our environment. Working with the Faeries and Elves can give us many blessings such as magical knowledge and power, wisdom of the natural environment, and to learn how to establish a deeper spiritual connection with our earth and her natural cycles. There is also much healing magick they can teach us. After all, natural medicines come from the earth and the Faeries and Elves can teach us how to use the healing magick of the earth for ourselves and the benefit of others.

Now, you may be asking, "How do I know if I am working with an Elf for a Fairy?" This is a very good question. As you recall from above, Elves and Faeries are very similar and perhaps the only real difference between them is their regional names. For example, is someone considered a Nordic or a Celtic? They are all still human and have similar traits but the only main difference is that they are from another country. So, when working with these beings if you are not sure which one is which, my advice is to simply ask. Personally, I have found that they are both very similar in magick and style and it really does not matter which being makes contact with you. The important thing is that the beings are willing to work with you and help you upon your spiritual path. For the rest of this chapter, the magical techniques I will give you are both for Faeries and Elves.

Where To Find Elves and Faeries

The literature and lore surrounding Elves and Faeries are full of descriptions of where to find them. They live in the "between" and we are able to find them there quite easily. The best time of day to find them is at dusk and dawn. These are times that are in between night and day. These times also play with light and shadows of the world. You would do well to meditate on the concepts of dusk and dawn for further gnosis on the subject. Another wonderful time for these beings is at the time of the full moon. Just as the full moon is a powerful time to see spirits and the dead, it is also a wonderful time to see the Elves and Faeries. The light of the full moon helps us see all entities that are in the world of Spirit and the Elves and Faeries are not exception. As for time of year, the two most powerful times are Beltane and Samhain, just we discussed above, as well as Imbolc, Lughnasadh, and Midsummer. These are times of the changing and in between times. Beltane is between spring and summer, Midsummer is the changing from the waxing to the waning sun, Lughnasadh is between summer and autumn, and Samhain is between autumn and winter. As for the Winter Solstice, I myself, take this a time to invite all spirits of the wood into my home for warmth and I will gladly work with the Elves and Faeries on this day as well as leave them Yuletide offerings.

There are also physical locations that you can go to work with the Elves and Faeries. They can be found in lonely forests, hill tops, rivers, streams, lakes, mountains, canyons, stones, trees, and many other things that are found in nature. Nature is their natural dwelling place but they can certainly live in homes and other places if they choose to. The Elves and Faeries do not necessarily live inside these things. I have rarely seen an Elf actually live in a tree. These places of nature are used as portals into the Otherworld where they live. The best way to connect with the Elves and Faeries is to journey out into the world of nature. The more isolated the better, but the witches who belong to my magical circle and I have certainly communed with the Elves out in a public park.

There are certain times of the year or personal circumstances that it may be difficult to travel to far off natural places. Sometimes the weather does not cooperate. Living in Chicago, there have been many Beltane and Samhain nights that have been either too cold or too rainy to hike into the forests. When this happens, you can certainly spiritually journey into the Otherworld using trance techniques in the comfort of your own home.

Connecting with Nature and The Otherworld

The best way to begin working with the Bright and Shining Ones is to go out into nature. These beings are a part of nature and help with the harmony of the land and Mother Earth. It is always better to go to where a spirit lives when beginning a new relationship. Ideally, you will want to find someplace that is secluded from human interaction. If at all possible, you should make a journey out into a deep forest, secluded mountains, or any place that is hardly touched by humans. That being said, it is sometimes difficult to find such a place easily. In Chicago, we are lucky enough to have a few forest preserves that are woodsy and almost untouched. However, I understand that not everyone has that opportunity to find such a place. Unfortunately, many people believe the earth is theirs to do with and are constantly destroying our natural environments. If you do not have a wild place in nature to go then we can make do with what we have. You can try to find a secluded public park, beach, desert, mountain, or grassy field. If you cannot go to such a place then you can set up a little natural area in your home or back porch. Get lots of plants, little trees, and flowers. The wilder like the better. The purpose here is to connect to nature to experience the Web of Wyrd and the Otherworld.

Once you have found your natural environment, there are a few things you will need to bring with you. You will need to bring offerings to the Shining Ones. Beer, Mead, Wine, Cakes, Honey, Milk and Bread are some of the most popular. If you need, you can bring a little blanket or cushion to sit on while in a trance state. Also make sure you are taking care of yourself. Bring appropriate clothes, jackets, and food and water if you like. If you are traveling very far you will be glad you brought these things. Also, I love incense. It makes me feel magical and puts me into trance very easily. Pick a scent that the Faeries and Elves will enjoy. Some good choices are sage, rose, jasmine, cedar, lavender, geranium, and any other floral scent.

1. Find a place in nature that you can do your work. Bring your offerings and other supplies needed.

2. Sit on the ground (you may use a chair, cushion, or blanket) and take a moment to settle in to the natural environment. Look around you. What do you see? What do you hear? What do you smell? What does the earth feel like under you?

3. Light your incense and allow yourself to get into a meditative trance state.

4. Close your eyes and connect with the natural energies around you. Imagine your head, heart, and skin are full of magical sensors that can sense magical energy. Breathe this natural energy into your body and just feel.

5. Visualize your aura around you. Now, expand your aura larger and larger until it expands around everything in your natural environment. Your aura should be large enough that the landscape and all of nature are within it. Take a moment to feel this connection with nature.

6. While maintaining this energetic connection, open your eyes and look around you. What do you see? Can you see the energies coming off the land? What are the animals doing around you? If you do not see energies, that is OK. Visualize earth energy coming from the land, the plants, the animals, the sky, and the rest of the environment.

7. As you visualize the earth energy, allow your consciousness to become one with the energies. You are connected to all things. You are a part of the land and the land is a part of you. There is no distinction between you and nature. You and nature are one. Take a moment to experience this.

8. Allow your consciousness to go deeper into the feeling of oneness. Tell yourself to connect to the Web of Wyrd. Take as much time as you need. Do not judge this experience.

Let it be what it is.

9. When you are ready, come back to your everyday consciousness. Take a few deep breaths and ground any excess energy.

10. Journal your experience.

Establishing a Relationship With The Shining Ones

When working magick with the Elves and Faeries it is important to establish a relationship with them. It will take them a while to learn to trust you and they will not work with you magically if they do not deem you trust worthy. Everyone's relationships with the Shining Ones is different and we work with them for different reasons. Personally, I work with them because I am a healer and I am learning Elvish healing magick which resonates with me because it's natural magick. But you may have your own reasons to work with them that are sacred and powerful to you. Some people work with them because they want to learn how to heal Mother Earth in a more personal and direct way. Some people may work with them because they have a deep kinship with plants, stones, and animals and they want to connect with these things in a way that only Elves and Faeries can teach. Another reason to work with them is for Elvish or Fairy magick. I have found that unless they have a fondness for you, they rarely teach humans their magick simply for the case for doing so. For the Elves and the Fey to teach us magick there is usually some benefit to them and to the land. This is just their way.

There are those that the Elves and Faeries favor. There are many reasons why this could be so. There are many stories of the Shining Ones kidnapping humans and taking them into the Otherworld. They do this sometimes because they wish to procreate with humans in order to bring their offspring into the physical world. There are also many stories about how they have a fondness for someone simply because they fall in love with them. There have been times that the Elves and Faeries have a fondness for someone because of their bloodlines. They live significantly longer than humans and also have long memories. If they felt that your ancestors were honorable and respected them and the land, they would remember this. They also remember if one of your ancestors helped them in some way. The Elves and Faeries respect honorable people very much.

For most of us, we have to earn the respect of the Elves and Faeries through good works and patience. As I have said before, they do not trust us. Many of the Shining Ones have no interest in humans and so have no interest in helping us. To gain their trust, one of the first things you should do is give them offerings. This is a lovely gesture that builds good faith. You should also spend time in nature as well. Use the previous exercise to connect to the land and the Web of Wyrd. The more you spend time in nature the more you will come to understand the cycles of the earth, the plants, and the resident animals. As witches and Spirit Walkers, we have to be connected to nature this is what gives us our magick. The more you are connected to nature, the more the Elves and Faeries will take notice of you. The last and yet most important thing is to have an open heart to them as well as a heart that wishes to heal the earth and connect to all of nature. To have a truly open heart means to want to reconnect to all life on earth for the betterment of the three worlds and all those beings we dwell within them.

Meeting The Elves and Faeries

There are several ways to meet the Elves and Faeries. One of the most common ways to meet them is through dreams. It is our gateway into the Otherworld. The Shining Ones may come into our dreams to give us messages and teachings. We can also journey to them. Just as we can journey into the Upperworld and the Underworld, we can journey into the Otherworld to meet with them. We can also meet with them by using ecstatic dance as well as shaking and swaying seidr techniques. I have used all of these techniques to meet with the Elves and the Faeries depending upon what I was doing. If I am working in my home on a cold winter's night, I will certainly journey to them. If I am out in nature, ecstatic dance or seidr are definitely a great way to go into trance to meet the Shining Ones. The main thing is that you must be in a trance. You may choose the trance technique that works best for you for the best situation, but you must be in trance. As we know, trance is what helps us alter our conscious perception to allow ourselves to see and experience the Otherworld.

Dreams

Dreams are a wonderful way of communing with the Shining Ones. Many people have spoken of having dreams with Elves, Faeries, the Ancestors and the divine. When we first begin dreaming with the Faeries and Elves, they may disguise themselves as birds and animals and we may not release we are speaking with them. Over time, we will begin to recognize their energy signature and we will see through their shapeshifting. If you perform the dream ritual to speak with the Shining Ones and you do not dream of them keep practicing. They will definitely know that you are calling to them but they may take a while to reveal themselves to you.

1. Prepare offerings of bread and honey, wine, mead, milk, or any other offerings you feel the Shining Ones will enjoy.
2. Spend a few moments speaking with the Elves/ Faeries and asking them to come to you in your dreams. Tell them your reasons why you would like to work with them.
3. As you lie down in your bed, take a few breaths and relax your body.
4. Visualize yourself in a lonely wooded forest or mountain

top. Continue this visualization as you drift off to sleep.

5. Upon awakening, write down your experience in your journal.

6. If you do not remember your dreams, write down any feelings you may have felt during the night and upon waking up.

7. Thank the Shining Ones. If you do not remember your dreams be sure you thank them. You may not remember the Elves/ Faeries but they were there.

Ecstatic Dance

Ecstatic dance is a valuable tool for contacting The Shining Ones. This is one of my all-time favorite techniques so I still use trance dance to this day. It is so much fun to do and since the Elves and Faeries love dance and music then we should definitely enjoy this trance technique. Dancing with this technique has the added benefit of giving off your own personal energy to help the Elves and Faeries manifest in the physical world.

1. State your intention to the Shining Ones that you would like to see and work with them.

2. Light your incense and play drumming, electronic music, or pagan chants. For seeing the Shining Ones, any music that is Faery like or makes you feel "enchanted" will work very well.

3. Begin your trance dance and incorporate the breathing trance techniques.

4. Open your heart chakra and your energies to the Otherworld and the energies of the Elves and Faeries.

5. When you are sufficiently in a trance, slow your trance dance down and look around you. Do you see the Shining Ones? Do you feel they are there?

6. Once you see them or feel they are there, speak with them for a while. If this is your first time meeting them,

introduce yourself. If not, speak with them as you normally would.

7. When you are ready, thank them for speaking with you and give your farewells.

8. Ground your energies and give offerings

9. Journal your experience.

Journeying

For this exercise, you can use your drum, rattle, or a drumming recording. Make sure you have your sage or other fumigation herb. You may also light incense that is appropriate for Elf and Fairy work. You may use sage, rose, lavender, rosemary, geranium, jasmine or another floral scent. You may adapt the visualization below from forest to fit the landscape in which you live.

1. Smudge yourself with your sage or any other herbs that are purifying. Smudge any working tools such as the drum or rattle as well.

2. Give an offering of incense or smudge to the four directions.

3. State your intention to meet with the Elves/ Faeries.

4. Use one of the astral techniques to travel to the Otherworld. Visualize yourself standing in front of the great world tree. Look up high and see it mighty branches extend up into the clouds and off into space. Look at the great trunk and see how it is so wide you cannot see either side of the trunk. Call upon your Spirit Animal.

5. Turn around facing away from the mighty tree trunk. See before you an ancient and deep forest. You can feel the earth energy and magick radiating from the trees.

6. Begin walking deeper and deeper into the forest (or landscape). Ask your Spirit Animal to direct you to the Shining Ones. Open your heart chakra and send the

desire out into the forest to meet an Elf/ Faery.

7.   After a while an Elf/ Faery should come up to you. Introduce yourself and tell him/her the reason you would like to connect. Spend some time getting to know each other. Remember, the Shining Ones are shapeshifters. They may appear as an animal, bird, ray of light, or mist. If any of these things appear speak to it just as you would any spirit.

8.   When you are ready, say your goodbyes and come back to your body.

9.   Leave an offering and journal your experience.

If you did not meet and Elf/ Faery on the first journey that is Ok. You have to earn their trust. Keep trying and keep leaving offerings for them. Sometimes it may help to sing them a song as an offering. They love music and may respond well to your song. You can choose any song that feels spiritual and magical to you.

Shaking and Swaying Seidr

This technique is better performed out in nature but it can be performed in your ritual space. You can light incense if you like.

1.   State your intention to meet with the Shining Ones.

2.   Perform the shaking and swaying seidr exercise.

3.   Allow yourself to go deeper and deeper into trance. Take deep breaths. With each breath allow yourself to go deeper and deeper into trance.

4.   As you shake and sway, allow your consciousness to connect to the energies of the land and the Otherworld. Begin to feel the Oneness of all things in nature. You are a part of nature and nature is a part of you. Connect to the life force and the Web of Wyrd.

5.   Ask the Elves/ Faeries to reveal themselves to you. Open your heart chakra and allow yourself to trust the ebb

and flow of nature. Continue to go deeper into your connection to nature.

6.   When the Shining One arrives spend some time speaking with him/ her and introduce yourself.

7.   Once you have a strong connection to the Elf/ Faery, you can either stop the seidr technique or you can slow it down to a nice slow sway to maintain the trance.

8.   When you are ready, say your goodbyes.

9.   Leave an offering and journal your experience.

Elf and Faery Healing Magick

Elves and Faeries have very powerful healing magick. Humans sometimes struggle with living in harmony with our environment and the Universe. We often see ourselves as the superior intelligence in the world. Lakota, as well as other indigenous teachings, tell us that humans are but one component in the cycles of Mother Earth. Many people in our modern society fall away from nature. We live in cities surrounded by pollution and loud unnecessary noises. We eat food with many toxic chemicals and have to filter our water. We also work stressful jobs and worry about how we are going to pay bills. Many of us have lost our connection to the healing properties of nature. We need help. If we ask the aide of the Shining Ones, they may be able to help us.

Elves and Faeries live harmoniously to the regenerative energies of nature. They are able to connect to the life force of the earth which promotes healing. Let us take a moment to discuss what healing is. Healing is bringing us back into *homeostasis* which essentially means bringing one back into balance. To be back into balance one must regenerate wounds so we may function to our full capabilities as well as live in harmony with all things. The earth's life force helps the plants, trees, minerals, and animals achieve homeostasis through its regenerative properties. As I have said many times in this chapter, Elves and

Faeries live in harmony with this life force and have incorporated these energies into their daily lives. Because of this, their healing power is very strong.

Because the Shining Ones live so close to the physical plane, even though they are a part of the Otherworld, they can have a synergistic effect on human life and well-being. Some teachers on Elf and Faery lore believe that while they can heal us through the regenerative process, humans can heal them through our physical earth energies as well as help them with their connection to certain spiritual elements. R. J. Stewart in his book *Earth Light: The Ancient Path To Transformation-Rediscovering the Wisdom of Celtic and Faery Lore* says:

"Faery beings, however, may have a limited relative cycle of Elements and can only balance by merging with other beings that have the missing elemental energy. This is the heart of the ancient faery partners or marriages: a human will find his or her weakest Element strengthened and vitalized by relationship with a faery being: the faery being finds the potential fivefold Elemental pattern through relationship with a human. To paraphrase one of the oldest traditions concerning relationships between humans and faery beings, we have the potential to redeem them, to give them a spiritual element or constituent which they do not have , while they have the potential to regenerate us, to realign our imbalanced energies in harmony with primal images and environmental and planetary consciousness."

When learning Elvish and Faery Healing Magick it is important that you find a Healing Teacher. Your Healing Teacher will give you far better healing and energy techniques than I ever could. Learning to be a healer is very personal and is different for everyone. Energy Healers are similar to each other but each of us has techniques and special gifts that are all our own. I could give you Elvish Healing techniques that I have learned, but I think it is far more powerful for you to work with your own teacher and discover your own healing techniques.

Finding Your Elvish/ Faerie Healing Teacher

For this exercise we will use the journeying technique but you can certainly adapt seidr or trance dance to do meet your teacher. Sometimes the Elf/ Faery teacher will want to spend some time with you teaching you wonderful things so you may not be able to hold the dance or shaking and swaying seidr for a long time. If you chose to do trance dance or seidr you can slow it down to where you are basically slowly swaying back and forth.

1. You may use your drum, rattle, or use a drumming recording.

2. Smudge yourself, your space, and any ritual tools with sage, mugwort, frankincense or any herb that makes you feel magical.

3. State your intention to meet an Elf or Faery Healing Teacher. Light incense that feels like it is from the Otherworld. You can use sage, rose, lavender, cedar, jasmine, amber, just to name a few.

4. Beginning drumming. Take a few deep breaths and allow yourself to go into a trance.

5. Visualize yourself at your Otherworld entrance. Visualize yourself walking into your entrance and finding yourself in the Otherworld.

6. Once in the Otherworld, ask your Spirit Animal to lead your to an Elf or Faery Teacher who is willing to work with you.

7. After your Spirit Animal has led you to the place where your teacher would be, state your intention to meet an Elf or Faery Healing Teacher. Open your heart chakra and wait for a response.

8. After some time has passed an Elf or Faery Healing

Teacher should appear. Spend some time getting to know each other and ask if the Shining One will be your Healing Teacher. If yes, ask him/ her what kinds of offerings they prefer and set up regular times to meet so that you may begin your healing teachings. If the answer is no ask him/ her to direct you to an Elf or Faery who is willing to teach you Healing Magick.

9. When you are ready, come back to your body. Ground the energy and leave offerings.
10. Journal your experience.

Elvish Healing

I would like to take a moment and teach you some of the Elvish Healing magick that I learned from my Elf Teacher. I am very grateful that my teacher gave me permission to teach this technique to the public. This healing technique draws upon the regenerative powers of the land energies as well as connecting to the Web of Wyrd. In essence, through the powers of the land, you are altering the strand of wyrd of the person you are healing. This technique can be used to heal yourself as well. Ideally, you should perform this technique in nature but you can do this in any space you like.

1. Take a few moments to bring yourself into center and find balance within yourself.
2. Allow yourself to go into a slight trance. You can use drumming, rattling, shaking and swaying seidr, ecstatic dance or breathing techniques.
3. Connect to the energies of all of nature. See how it feels to be part of all of the natural creation of the earth.
4. Connect to the Web of Wyrd. Visualize the web that connects all things together.
5. Have the intention to alter the strand of wyrd only to heal. Not to alter the strand any further than that. It is

true you are altering the person's fate by connecting to the Web of Wyrd, but from my point of view, anytime you use energy healing for another you are altering their fate.

6.   Call upon your Elvish or Faery teacher to help guide you.
7.   Breath in the regenerating and healing energies of the earth into your heart chakra. As you exhale, send this energy down through your arms and out of your hands into the person you are healing. Visualize this earth energy cleansing, balancing, and regenerating the affliction in the person you are healing. If you are healing yourself, simply send the earth energy to the afflicted area of the body. If you are unsure what body part is afflicted you can send the energy into the heart chakra and allow the heart to send it to where it needs to go.
8.   When you are ready, disengage from the healing energy and the Web of Wyrd. Center and ground yourself.
9.   Journal your experience.

Faery Doctoring

Faerie Doctoring is a powerful form of healing. A Faerie Doctor is someone who has the ability to see Faeries and other spiritual beings and has the magical skill to heal spiritual ailments. Some believe that Faery Doctors received their skills at birth while others believe that they travel to the Otherworld in order to receive their training from the Faeries themselves. When someone has transgressed against the Elves or Faeries, many times, they will place a curse or other form of magick to attack the victim. The symptoms of Faerie Curse could be anything from a run of "bad luck", to elf shot, to becoming very sick. The Shining Ones are not known to curse any old random person, almost always, there was something that a person did that somehow offended them. There are many tales of Faeries cursing people for cutting down sacred trees, being rude or inhospitable to them, spying on them, destroying or building things on sacred land, going back on your word to them, and any other thing that they may find disrespectful or rude.

Faerie Doctors will employ their magical skills to ascertain if the person is, indeed, cursed by the Faeries. They may be able to see spiritual energies surrounding the victim or employ divination about the matter at hand. If it is determined that victim us not afflicted by Faery magick then they will be recommended to a regular doctor. But if it is found that the Faeries are responsible for the magick then the Faery Doctor will do all that they can for the person. Faery Doctoring itself varies from doctor to doctor depending upon their training. They may give the afflicted person a magical tea or potion to drink or provide them with magical charms and rituals to rid themselves of the malady. There are not many Faery Doctors nowadays, but there are those of us who have received healing instruction from Faerie Healers and Teachers and can help the poor souls who have offended the Faeries. If you are interested in becoming a Faery Doctor, ask your Faery Healing Teacher to teach you this wonderful art.

Treating Elf Shot

Elves rarely shoot humans with their magical arrows. When they do, it is usually because you have trespassed on sacred land or you have damaged their home in some way. If you are in an area of nature and you feel that you are not supposed to be there, that may be the Elves, Faeries, or nature spirits telling you that you are not welcome. When this happens, you should find another spot to be in. Living in an urban city, I cannot tell you how many times I have gone to a park or nature area and it is filled with litter; soda cans, plastic bags, plastic wrappers, paper plates, etc. It makes me angry quite frankly. Whenever I do any ceremony in nature, I try to always bring a little trash bag with me to clean up the area. The Elves love that. I wonder, sometimes, how many times someone has been elf shot because of their selfish behavior of polluting natural environments. If you think you have been a victim of elf shot, pay attention to the symptoms: aching pain in the affected area, swelling, wasting away in the area, skin diseases, and/or a rush of bad luck. It is relatively easy for the Spirit Walker to remove elf shot. Removing the magical arrow is similar to removing a spirit intrusion in shamanic way.

Find the afflicted area.

1. Using psychic focus, visualize what the elf arrow looks like.
2. Grab firmly on the arrow. It may be invisible to the physical eye, but you can touch it energetically. You may feel a vibration, tingly sensation, or a powerful force. Do not worry, the shaft of the arrow is not harmful, just the elf arrow.
3. Pull the arrow out of the body and firmly throw it into the ground. This will ground the energy and the arrow will dissipate.
4. Send healing energy to the wounded area. If the elf shot has been lodged in the victim for some time, there may be severe symptoms. Use the Elvish Healing Technique given previously to heal wounded area.
5. Leave an offering to the elves and ask their forgiveness of whatever grievance they have of you. Elves very much appreciate apologies and niceties like this. This rebuild trust between you and them.

Chapter 9

Dragon Magick

To Change, you must face the dragon of your appetites with another dragon: the life-energy of your soul. Rumi

There are many myths and legends that speak of fierce and mighty dragons. In many European tales they have the power to breathe fire and can cause great destruction. In Asian countries, dragons are often times benevolent beings who bring the fertile rains and can grant us good fortune. There are many different types of dragons, each with their own special magick. All too often, powerful beings are misunderstood and feared. People have the habit of demonizing things that hold great power. Dragons are the spiritual presence of what is called *serpent energies* in the Universe. Serpent energies are powerful forces that flow or spiral much like a flowing river. The dragon energies of creation and destruction keep the Universe in balance.

Dragons are found throughout the world and the cosmos. The three shamanic worlds are the homes of three great cosmic dragons. The Upperworld contains the mighty celestial dragon, Draco. Draco majestically sits between the Big Dipper and the constellation of Hercules. From our point of view on earth, she only takes up a small portion of the night sky, but in actuality, she is several light years in length. Our Milky Way can be considered a giant dragon as well. The arms of the Milky Way spiral in great beauty and power. This great cosmic energy of our galaxy spirals in such a way similar to a flying dragon. In Nordic mythology, there is a magnificent dragon, named Nidhogg who inhabits the Underworld and chews upon the roots of the shamanic world tree known as Yggdrasil. Nidhogg is the great dragon who rules the part of the Underworld where the spirits of the dishonored are kept. In Nordic myth, there is a squirrel who runs up and down the tree exchanging insults between Nidhogg and the great Upperworld eagle. Perhaps in Nordic cosmology, the cosmic eagle is a higher vibration of the dragon. The Midworld is the home of the giant Nordic serpent named Jormungandr, who encompasses the whole earth. This great serpent is the energy that keeps the earth from collapsing upon itself in total destruction. There is a tale how Thor, the god of thunder, caught the great dragon on a fishing expedition and had a great battle. In the end, Jormungandr was released and the world was saved.

Dragons, seen in the land as serpent lines, are the regenerative forces of the earth. Not only do they contain the energies of the land, seas, and skies, but they are the powers of the evolving earth itself. Li-lung is a class of dragon in China that dwells in the earth and water. Ernest Ingersoll, in his book *Dragons and Dragon Lore* says:

> "As the earth-dragon, Li is supposed to exist beneath the surface, and to cause earthquakes by uneasy movements of its gigantic frame; and in one case…caused a great landslide, which partly dammed the Yangtse and formed the dread rapids in the gorge above Ichang, called the Dragon's Gate."

As humans, we have a tendency to try to "tame" the forces of nature. We can find ourselves believing that technology can somehow change our environment so that nature does not affect us. As we are learning now, the pollution from technology that comes from factories is causing climate change. I believe that climate change is the dragons' response against our attempt to tame and control the earth's natural resources. There has been a great increase of earthquakes, hurricanes, storms, fires, and volcanic eruptions. Could this be one of the roots of the myth of dragons destroying man-made structures? There are several stories and myths of the European dragon destroying land, homes, and livestock. One story from the Ukraine relates how the dragon, Tugarin, wreaked havoc throughout the land. "Tugarin made himself a plague on the countryside, stealing livestock, burning buildings, and slaying all who tried to do him in." Doug Nile, *Dragons: The Myths. Legends, and Lore.*

The purpose of establishing a relationship with dragons and doing magick with them is because they are the spirits of the moving energies of the earth and of nature. They are very ancient creatures and are very powerful. Dragons have many abilities such as the power to help us heal the land and ourselves. The very nature of the dragon's fiery breath is that of transformation. Fire transforms one thing into another. It burns away the old, changing the chemical composition of the object, and creates something new. Because dragons are ancient, they are very wise and can help us on our spiritual path. Dragons are sometimes seen as gods, angels, or immortals. In my research, and, of course, my relationship with them, I have found that they are not immortal, yet can live hundreds and even thousands of years. Yes, it is true that they protect treasure. This treasure is not the gold of legends in myth, but the gold of wisdom and enlightenment as well as the secrets of the earth's regenerative force. Dragons will guard this ancient treasure with their lives. Only the witch and Spirit Walker who works toward spiritual development may obtain the dragon's treasures of magick, enchantment, and spiritual enlightenment. They are the flowing energies of the land, as long as they land is alive, then too, will the dragon be alive. The two are synergistic. What affects the land affects the dragon and what affects the dragon affects the land. They are also the keepers of magick, wisdom, and enchantment. They can teach us how to have a better relationship with the land and all those beings, be it animal or spirit, who live upon the land.

The Serpent Lines of Earth: Ley Lines

Ley lines, sometimes called "earth meridians", are lines of energy that travel upon the earth's surface. It may be helpful to think of these energy lines like rivers of energy. Rivers flow water from their origin to their destination. Rivers carry rushing water through the countryside. Similarly, ley lines carry currents of earth energy from the point of origin to its destination. The energy from ley lines brings life force from deep in the earth, to the rocks, soil, plant life, and animals. The energy from these lines keeps the vitality of the earth balanced and thriving. When the energy from the ley lines are flowing the environment thrives. Trees and plants grow to be very large, animals are abundant, and the magick is strong. There is the feeling of balance and wellbeing, When the energy of the ley lines is weak, the environment is also weak. Plants and animals do not thrive and the energy of the landscape feels negative or uneasy. Even though the popularity of ley lines may have originated in Britain, they can be found all over the world.

When we look at ley lines and spirit roads with psychic focus, we can see how the energies move down these paths in a twisting and winding motion that resembles a great serpent or a dragon. To the witch and Spirit Walker, it appears as though a dragon was moving with the energetic currents of the land. The earth has many of these ley lines and spirit roads, so therefore, there are many dragons. Ley lines are not the only places of the earth where dragons can be found. Dragons are energy. Wherever life force and energy flows forth or pools together, a dragon most likely can be found. There are dragons of the land, mountains, rivers, lakes, and oceans. In Chinese mythology, dragons often take the form of clouds, rain, and streams.

In 1922, Alfred Watkins was one of the first people of the modern era to search for ley lines. He believed that it was relatively simple to track ley lines if one had a simple map. Once you have a general understanding of the land in question you could make marks on your map with certain natural and manmade structures. He understood that ancient pagans built grave mounds, sacred sites, standing stones and many other things to harness the power of the ley lines. Once you marked your map with these sacred landmarks you could take the straight edge of something such as a ruler and draw straight lines that intersect these sites.

In his book, *The Old Straight Track: Its Mounds, Beacons, Moats, Sites, and Mark Stones,* Alfred Watkins give his list of possible sites to pay special attention to:

1. Ancient mounds
2. Ancient unworked stones
3. Moats, and islands in ponds or lakelets
4. Traditional or holy wells
5. Beacon points
6. Cross-roads with place names, and ancient wayside crosses.
7. Churches of ancient foundation, and hermitages
8. Ancient castles, and old "castle" place-names.

Alfred maintained that whenever you find standing stones, earthworks, and ancient sacred sights they were surely on a ley line. He believed that the Neolithic people knew how to harness the power of the leys with these sacred constructions.

Ley lines are found all over the world. One could say that the Egyptian pyramids, Aztec pyramids, Northern European burial mounds, and Native American mounds and structures were built upon ley lines. They key to finding ley lines is with lining up these spiritual structures with the natural landscape. Mountains, rivers, lakes, rocks, trees, and hills are all good indicators of ley lines. Naturally, not all of the landscape is on a ley line, but if it lines up with ancient structures, there is a good chance it may be.

Alfred Watkins discovered that where two ley lines crossed

there as an amazing amount of power:

> "Where more than two ley lines cross at one point it is probably (and where more than three cross it is certain) that the point has become an initial point for originating all after the first two. Stonehenge, for example, first had its site decided by the crossing of leys, then the sun temple built on a mark stone, which then became the initial point from which other leys were sighted."

Throughout history, we see that anytime two roads meet there is a powerful force or vortex. The Greco-Roman Hecate is the goddess of crossroads. She has power over witchcraft and opening the veil to the Underworld. In Vodou, there is Papa Legba, the god of the crossroads. Papa Legba is called to open the way between this world and the spirit world. In his book *The Haitian Vodou Handbook: Protocols for Riding the Lwa,* Kanaz Filan says:

> "Legba is the first one saluted at any Vodou ceremony. Because he is the keeper of the gateway, no spirit can enter the peristyle without his permission. He is the one who facilitates communication with the spirit world."

In Traditional Witchcraft, the crossroads is where we meet the horned one, sometimes called the Devil or the Man in Black. It is here, witches do great works of magick, consult the dead, and speak with The Master himself.

> "...he is the Devil wrestled in the Churchyard for the Toad Bone, the Black Man at the crossroads who grants us our greatest desire, the Trickster who fools us into thinking the Path of Fate we walk is one we 'chose'", Peter Paddon, *A Grimoire For Modern Cunning Folk.*

Standing stones placed along ley lines had a similar function to Chinese acupuncture. If we consider for a moment that the ley lines were the earth's version of the human body's energy meridians then the stones were similar to acupuncture needles. The stones helped focus, direct, and channel the earth lines. Standing stones were thought to have always been placed at the place where leys crossed each other. It is believed that the standing stones in Britain and Europe were used by pagans and healers to perform magick. It was also believed that the standing stones could grant healing as well give an energy boost to any ceremony you were to perform.

Ley lines were also considered haunted with spirits. The earth meridians were power sources for the dead to come to and from the Underworld. These lines were called spirit roads, ghost paths, or faery tracks. Some may argue that ley lines and spirit roads are not the same thing. From my perspective with working with both ley lines and spirit roads, I have found that spirit roads are a smaller version of ley lines. I like to think of it like ley lines are rivers and spirit roads are little streams that shoot out from them. Likewise, when we once again compare leys to the energy channels of the body, ley lines are the Chinese meridians and spirit roads are similar to nadis, energy channels in the body that function how capillaries function in the body.

For now, we will call these smaller energy channels spirit roads. There are many tales about spirit roads. Some say that they are straight while others say they are crooked. I have seen these roads to be both. The crooked road makes more sense to me because in Traditional Witchcraft we say we are "walking the crooked path". Spirit roads seem to be more predominate in rural areas. Often times, we find ourselves traveling these same roads in our everyday lives so you may often see the grass or fields warn with foot traffic or even small country roads. In old rural towns there is a road called "the corpse road". This is the path from the church to the cemetery. It can be as small as a few feet to several miles. It is said that at night you may see ghostly funerals walking the corpse road. Sometimes witches will watch the procession to see who is in the casket. For this foretells whose death is coming. Ghost Roads serve a similar function as corpse roads, but are generally not for the recently or soon to be dead, but are a road that is in constant use for the spirits of the dead.

Faery Tracks are the paths that the fey take on their nightly procession. They are more or less straight until they reach a marker such as a sacred tree, stone, or some other natural object. It is said that a home should never be built on a Faery track because you are interrupting their procession and will cause ill luck for all those who live within. W. Y. Evans-Wentz, in his book *The Fairy-Faith in Celtic Countries,* says:

"If a house happens to be built on a fairy preserve, or in a fairy track, the occupants will have no luck. Everything will go wrong. Their animals will die, their children fall sick, and no end of trouble will come on them. When the house happens to have been built on a fairy track, the doors on the front and back, or the windows if they are in line with the track, cannot be kept closed at night, for the fairies must march through."

I grew up in a rural town outside of Houston, Texas. Behind our home was a patch of woods that grew on either side of an old trail. Many of the farmers would take their dead livestock such as horses, cows, goats, cats, and dogs and simply toss them in those old woods. They would also discard old large appliances like washing machines, dryers, and refrigerators back in these same woods. Because of these two things, we called that area Dead Man's Alley. I spent most of my childhood back in those woods. I was fascinated with the process of decay and the bones that were left behind. Most importantly, it was haunted. During the day, you always felt like you were being watched by the spirits. A few times when I was little, I would see strange creatures staring back at me as I walked alone. There were stories about people being murdered back there, but they were just stories. I think. Many people who lived close to Dead Man's Alley had strange things or bad luck happen to them. The man who lived in the house right next to it tried to kill his wife one night. Thankfully he did not succeed. Once, when I was a teenager, I found myself walking along the paths just as the sun set and darkness fell upon the woods. My brothers and I knew never to be in those old woods after dark. We do not know how we knew; we just did. As I started walking home on the dark path, the winds picked up and I could hear rustling in the brush along the path. Just then, I heard the loud sounds of a giant boar with hooved feet. There are no wild boars in that part of Texas. Startled, I ran home as fast as I could. It is funny the speed you can run when you know something otherworldly may be after you. As a grown-up pagan, I came to understand that Dead Man's Alley was a faery track or ghost road. Maybe both. Either way, I know first-hand of both the beauty and the danger of living near such a fantastic thing.

Chinese Dragon lines

The Chinese have known about earth energy lines for thousands of years. Feng shui is the art of locating these energy lines that they call *dragon lines*. Feng Shui means "wind and water." In this practice, energy lines are compared to the meridians of Traditional Chinese Medicine. In his book *Feng Shui: The Living Earth Manual*, Stephen Skinner says:

"Ch'i flows through the earth like an underground stream that varies its course according to the seasons and the changes made by nature or man to the surface of the earth...A parallel can be drawn with the flow of ch'i through the acupuncture meridians of the body. These meridians are not the same as blood vessels that can be dissected with the surgeon's knife, but convey the life energy through their own specific and precisely locatable channels."

There are experts in terrestrial Feng Shui called "dragon men". These men find the source of earth energy lines and harnesses its energy and power for the fertility and betterment of the land and its people. It is also believed that the cultivating of the dragon lines increases health, prosperity, and luck. Dragon men are experts at finding the dragon within the land. Once this is done, they are able to find the ch'i that is pooled from the dragon that is beneficial for the surrounding land. In Feng shui, the most ch'i is found around the dragon's heart and genitals. The feet and tail have the least amount of ch'i.

There are many forms of ch'i. There is the life force of the human body. This maintains our health. If our ch'i is out of balance then we become sick. When our ch'i is healthy and flowing correctly we have good health and balance. There is also celestial ch'i. This is the energy of the stars, planets, galaxies, and the moon. Earth ch'i is the energy of the earth that maintains the health of the landscapes and environment. All of these different types of ch'i affect our health and happiness. In Feng shui, it is believed that the energy of the environment and the land in which we live affects our inner happiness and peace. In essence, if the energy of the land is healthy and happy then you will be happy and healthy as well. This is an important consideration in our modern-day life. Living in toxic areas of pollution and violence not only has an effect on our physical health, it also has an energetic and spiritual effect on us as well.

Dragon men have the ability to detect the dragon lines of the earth and determine if they are in harmony with the natural landscape. Like landscape artists, they design the land in such a way that brings together good healthy earth ch'i while sending away unhealthy ch'i. They do this by deciding the proper place for trees, bushes, ponds, pools, and other natural items as they relate to the dragon lines. When healthy, dragon lines bring good fortune, health, and happiness. This healthy earth energy not only benefits the living, but it also benefits the ancestors of the land. Remember, it was not until the modern era that our ancestors were buried far away from out home. To the ancient Chinese, it was an honor to have your ancestors nearby. The beneficial energies of the dragon lines also fed the ancestors good energy. This, in turn, was beneficial for the living. In my book *Deeper Into The Underworld: Death, Ancestors, and Magical Rites* I talk about how the more powerful your ancestors become with energies, offerings, and prayers, the more magick and healing they are able to give you and your family.

As it is related to the land, the Chinese dragon can physically be seen in the land itself. The hills and the terrain are the body of the dragon while the rivers and underground waters are the dragon's blood. When looking at a map or aerial view of the land, it may be easier to see the dragon's body in the shape of the land and the mountains. Dragons are also found in waterways. To the Chinese dragon men, they can find the home of the dragons, not only in and on top of mountains, but in waterways as well. When two natural bodies of water meet there is a dragon. For example, when a river and a lake meet there lives a dragon. Also, when a river or stream naturally curves this is a good indication of where a dragon lives. Weather in an important feature in ch'i and Chinese dragons. When water begins to evaporate and flow into the sky, this is the dragon taking the form of water vapor. The dragon then takes the form of clouds until enough water vapor has built up within the dragon cloud. Once this happens, the water takes the form of rain and waters the mountains, rivers, and the land once more. This is the transformation of the dragon. He is able to transform himself into water vapor, clouds, and then back to the land once more. These dragons bring waters of healing and fertility to the earth. They bring the good ch'i to us that may seem like good luck.

The Personal Dragon-Kundalini

Many modern spiritual philosophies teach that each person is a reflection of the Universe. We are made up of the light of the stars, the body of the earth, and spirit of the divine. We carry our ancestral blood and karma in our DNA. We also have our spirit helpers who guides us on our spiritual path. As we have seen in a previous chapter, we also have our connection to the animal world and our animal self through our Spirit Animal. We also have our own personal dragon. This is the serpent energy that lies asleep at the base of our spines at our sacrum. In tantric teachings of India, this is known as *kundalini.* Kundalini in Sanskrit means "coiled up" and is energetically seen as a serpent coiled up three times at the base of our spines with its tail in its mouth. This personal dragon can aid us in strengthening our magical powers as well as enhancing our connection to the dragons of the earth. In order to do this, we must awaken the kundalini energy so she can rise up the spine empowering each chakra until she unites with our crown chakra. In his book, *Kundalini: The Arousal of the Inner Energy,* Ajit Mookerjee says:

"The Kundalini Shakti or 'coiled feminine energy' is the vast potential of psychic energy, the body's most powerful thermal current. The arousal of Kundalini is not unique to tantric practice, but forms the basis of all yogic disciplines, and every genuine spiritual experience may be considered a flowering of this physio-nuclear energy."

In tantra, the coiled serpent is seen as the goddess Shakti and the crown chakra is the god Shiva. In kundalini meditation, the goddess climbs her way up the spine seeking union with her beloved Shiva. Their union empowers, heals, and strengthens the tantric. I think that this is a beautiful way to imagine the kundalini energies but the Hindu gods are not our focus for this exercise. Remember, the Tantrics saw these energies through their cosmological lens and it has powerful meanings for them. For us, I think it is more powerful and affirming to see the energies to our own cosmological lens of the dragon energy that dwells in each of us. The coiled serpent who lies sleeping in the sacrum, at the root chakra, is the earth dragon. This is the fiery earth dragon who seeks union with the cosmos. The energy at the crown chakra is the Upperworld dragon, sometimes seen as the constellation of Draco. When the earth dragon travels up the spine, she cleanses, strengthens, and unlocks the power of the chakras. When she reaches the Upperworld dragon, they combine to form the alchemy of magick of the dragon. The union of both earth and celestial force that creates healing and magick within the body.

There are many ways to awaken the personal dragon. One way is to sit in meditation and "aliven" the dragon through breath, visualization, and the intonation of sound. When the personal dragon wakes up, she is then impowered further through the breath. Then, you must visualize her flying up into each of the chakras. Again, the Tantrics used intonations that are sacred to them and have special meaning that resonates with Hindu cosmology. You certainly can use those chakra mantras if you are so inclined, but it is not necessary. Instead you can vibrate words or simple sounds that are powerful to you. You can intone and vibrate the words "Awaken", "Arise", "Harmony", or any other word that makes you feel like the dragon energy is cleansing and strengthening each chakra. Another way to awaken the personal dragon is to dance or to use the shaking and swaying seidr techniques. In this next exercise I will teach you how to awaken the personal dragon with dance.

Dancing the Dragon

1. Review the Trance Dance exercise. Make sure you practice the exercises before attempting to awaken your personal dragon.

2. Find music that you prefer. You may choose tribal, chant, or electronic dance. Make sure the music has no lyrics. You may light incense if you like. Dragon's blood, frankincense, rosemary, cinnamon, or another fiery incense will work well.
3. Begin to move your feet to the rhythm. Take deep breaths and begin to send the breath to the serpent asleep at your sacrum.
4. Start moving your hips. As you do this breath in fiery energy to the dragon and see her begin to awaken. Keep moving your hips to the music until she feels sufficiently awake. You will know because your sacrum will feel heated. Visualize the dragon inside the root chakra. See her cleanse, strengthen, and empower the chakra simply by her magical presence. You may intone a word if you like such as "Awaken" or "Rise".
5. As you move your hips, now add moving your belly to the music. See the dragon move up to the naval chakra to cleanse, strengthen, and empower. Take a moment and enjoy this feeling.
6. Begin to move your chest and upper torso. See the dragon move up to the solar plexus. See her cleanse, strengthen, and empower the chakra.
7. Move your arms and shoulders to the music. See the dragon move to your heart chakra to cleanse, strengthen, and empower.
8. Move your neck and head to the music. See the dragon move to your throat chakra to cleanse, strengthen, and empower.
9. Continue to move your head and neck as well as the rest of your body to the music. See the dragon move to your brow chakra to cleanse, strengthen and empower.
10. Finally, see the dragon move to your crown chakra. See her join in union with the Upperworld chakra of the crown.

Allow yourself to experience this alchemical union of the earth dragon and the celestial dragon. See the energy flow up through the crown and then the energy showers down upon your body in healing magical energy.

11. End the trance dance when you are ready. Slow the dance down and feel the earth dragon descend back down the chakras and return to the root chakra.

12. Ground any excess energy and journal your experience.

If you perform the personal dragon meditation dance and you cannot get the dragon to go all the way up to the crown chakra that is okay. There are a few reasons this may occur. One, and the most common, is that there are energetic blocks in that chakra that need to be removed. When this happens, all you need to do is keep practicing. Just like running or lifting weights, you may have to work your way up to it. Another reason could be that it is very distracting to dance and visualize at the same time. Again, keep practicing, you will get there. If you like, you can simply sit and do this same exercise, but I have found it more powerful if you engage your whole body. This is one of those magical exercises that is fun as well as powerful. Keep practicing and enjoy the experience!

Meeting The Dragon

To begin working with dragons you must establish a relationship with them. They are powerful magical creatures and are not so much concerned with the affairs of humans. Their purpose is to maintain the energies and the structure of the land. They are part of the earth's Web of Wyrd and an important part of its vitality and well-being. When humans begin harming the earth, then the dragons will cleanse the land so that it can heal. This is maybe one of the reasons why tornados, earthquakes, and tidal waves destroy the structures that people have created. It may be that the dragon energies are manifesting as weather phenomenon to cleanse harmful things away from the earth. Keeping this idea in mind, perhaps this is why dragons burn down houses and destroy villages in mythology and lore. I would like to take a moment and talk about the nature of dragons. As we have said before, they are the wild untamed forces of nature and the land. They are not good nor bad, they simply are who they are. We cannot change the nature of dragons just as we cannot tame the nature of a shark, a wolf, or a lion. Many have tried, but eventually the primal nature of the beast always strikes out.

When we approach dragons, we do so with reverence, humility, and caution. For hundreds of years, dragons have watched as we have polluted and destroyed the land. We have dumped chemicals in the land and dug out her earth looking for jewels, metals, coal and many other things. We have drained water ways for homes and roads and cleared forests for livestock. Dragons do not trust us, and rightly so. We have not been trustworthy to the earth and her creatures. If we are going to establish a relationship with dragons, we must earn back their trust. We do so by taking care of the land. Recycle, reuse, plant trees, and give honor to the Earth Mother herself. We should help them understand that our goal is to work with the spirits of the land and to heal the earth. This may take time. Dragons can see the energies of our auras and they know what our intentions are. If you approach them simply for power, then you will be ignored. If you approach them with reverence and an open heart, you just may get their attention.

When we begin to work with the dragons for magick it is important to have one main dragon that you work with, but you may work with several. This is not unlike your Otherworld guide, but rather than a guide it is your "ambassador" if you will. This dragon will help you learn about their nature as well as their powerful magick. He or she will teach you how to approach other dragons and what kind of offerings they like. They will teach you much magick and most importantly, how to take care of the land and the nature spirits who live upon the land, under the land, and fly over the land. It is important to get to know the dragon you work with. Ask him or her their name, but do not be offended when they do not give it to you. You have to earn their trust. They may give you a name to use that may or may not be their true name. Dragons know of the magical law that states to know something's name is to have power over it. So, do not be surprised if a dragon gives you a different name then their true name. Be respectful and say thank you. If at all possible, you will need to go to a natural spot closest to your home to find your dragon. If you do not have access to a place in nature where dragons are normally found, they you may go outside and use the land as it is. If you live in a city, you may go to a park for your magick. Ideally, find a place that you will not be disturbed. There are dragon energies everywhere. Witches have the ability to seek out the serpent lines in order to find dragons. In her book *Traditional Witchcraft: A Cornish Book of Ways,* Gemma Gary says:

"Detecting and harnessing the serpentine flow is of great importance to the Pellar, and they must know the ways to this and the places where this force will be best drawn forth. The desire to seek these energies and draw upon them, and indeed the ability to do so, should be naturally held within the true witch."

Journey To The Dragon

1. Find a local spot in nature where a dragon would be. You can go to a river, lake, mountains, hills, mountains, forests, or any place that is in nature.
2. Sit upon the earth. If you would like to drum or rattle all the better. You can sing a song or simply use your rattle or drum.
3. Take a moment and sense the dragon below you in the land. Send a tendril of your energy to the dragon. Allow

the dragon to feel your energy. He or she may send you energy back. If not, that is ok, the dragon is aware of your presence.

4. Journey down to the dragon's lair using one of the astral projection techniques.

5. Take a moment to see the dragon. What does he/ she look like? How big or small is it? Is it sleeping or awake? Sometimes dragons may sleep through the winter months.

6. Introduce yourself to the dragon. He/ she may or may not tell you their name. Spend some time getting to know the dragon.

7. When you are finished, come back to your body. Leave an offering of flowers, wine, or food. Make sure anything that is left is biodegradable.

8. Spend some time each day getting to know the dragon. This is an opportunity for him/ her to get to know you. Eventually, you will begin to earth the dragon's trust.

The Dragon's Breath

One of the most unique aspects of the dragon is its fiery breath. The dragon's breath burns and destroys everything in its path. No armor or magick can stand up to the power of the fire breath. For this reason, we will use the dragon's breath to ward and protect our home and magical space. I would advise performing this simple ceremony every night to protect your home from malefic magick, magical attacks, or unwanted spirits and entities entering your home. You can also use this ceremony to protect your ritual space before magical workings. For this spell, we will use a combination of smoke and fire-the dragon's breath. You will need a fireproof container. A small iron cauldron works well, but any fireproof container will do. You will also need charcoal for incense, dragon's blood resin or any other herb or incense that has a fiery quality.

1. Place the charcoal in your fireproof container and light.
2. Send your consciousness down under the earth and call upon your dragon that you have been working with.
3. Place your dragon's blood, or other incense, upon your charcoal and say, **"I call upon you great dragon to protect my home (magical space) from all those beings magical or physical who wish me harm. Protect this space from top to bottom, from side to side, and from within and without."**
4. As the incense begins to smoke walk counter-clockwise from the front door all around your home and then back to the front door. As you do so, visualize the great dragon coming from beneath the earth and into the charcoal and smoke.
5. Visualize the incense smoke as the dragon's fiery breath. As the smoke flows to the walls and ceiling, see the dragon breathe its fiery breath around your entire home. Visualize a the dragon fire encompassing your home. The dragon will protect your home as if it were its own.
6. If you are using this technique to protect your ritual space, simply walk with the dragon fumigation around your circle. Visualize your space encompassed by a sphere of dragon fire.
7. Give the remaining incense to the dragon as a sacred offering, **"Great dragon, please accept this incense as an offering."**

Invoking Dragon Energy

One of the most intimate and yet powerful magical techniques is invocation. Invocation is the power to take in energy, spirits, gods, or ancestors into your body. There are many reasons why we would want to invoke. It is a wonderful way to commune and share energies with a spirit. Another reason is that the spirit can manifest in your body in order to perform great works of magick. In Solomon's style of ceremonial magick, the way to control chthonic spirits is by invoking the Bornless One, or God, into your body. By doing this, you are entering a synergistic relationship with the creator. You give him a body to manifest and he gives you a portion of his power to do your Will.

When we invoke the dragon into our body, the dragon energies will merge with our own. We will have a better understanding its energies and he/ she will have a better understanding of our energies. During invocation, the dragon's consciousness will merge with our own. This will give us the rare opportunity to know a small sliver of the dragon's thoughts, desires, and greater purpose. In this particular invocation, we are not allowing ourselves to become possessed. We are allowing a small part of the dragon consciousness within ours. You have control over your body and your mind. The dragon cannot possess you unless you allow it. Until you have established a firm relationship, do not allow this to occur.

Dragon Invocation

This technique can be performed inside, but it is more powerful outside in nature. In order to invoke the dragon, you will use the shaking and swaying technique.

1. Go to the place in nature where your Dragon Guide lives.
2. Perform the shaking and swaying seidr technique.
3. As you perform the shaking and swaying seidr technique, send your consciousness down into the earth to where your Dragon Guide lives.
4. Explain to your dragon your intention to invoke them and ask your dragon to enter into your body.
5. Continue to shake and sway. Take long deep breaths and, with your mind and your energies, bring the dragon's energies up through the ground.
6. The energies will enter your body through your feet,

up the legs, up into your torso, and into your head. Feel the fiery dragon energy pulsing with the fires of life and magick. With each breath, the dragon energies go higher and higher into your body until the dragon enters your head. Allow the dragon to join with your mind.

7. Allow the dragon's consciousness to merge with yours. Keep in mind that this is not a full possession. Allow the dragon to see through your eyes. To hear with your ears, and to experience sensations with your body.

8. You have full control of your mind and body but you are sharing it with dragon consciousness.

9. Spend a few moments with the dragon energy in your body. If the energy is too strong ask the dragon to dampen the energies.

10. Ask the dragon what magick and power you can do with this invocation. Spend some time in conversation with the dragon.

11. When you are ready, thank the dragon and send it back to its dwelling. Disengage the dragon's consciousness with yours. Feel the energies going back down through your body and back into the ground.

12. Leave offerings to the dragon. Journal your experience.

The Voices of Animals

In the *Saga of the Volsungs,* there is the story of Sigurd and the dragon, Fafnir. In the tale, Fafir was a man who killed his own father because he wanted his great wealth of gold. He hoarded the gold and became more greedy and isolated day by day until Fafnir transformed into a giant dragon. Sigurd was given a sword from a man named Regin, who was the brother of Fafnir. Sigurd went off to kill the great dragon. Regin suggested that Sigurd dig a ditch and hide in it so that he could kill Sigurd. But Odin appeared in the disguise of an old man and told Sigurd that he should dig several ditches for the blood to run into. Sigurd did as instructed. Fafnir came out of his lair and walked mightily upon the earth. Sigurd, hiding in one of the ditches, plunged his sword into the belly of Fafnir. The blood poured into the ditches and the dragon died. Regin asked Sigurd to cook the heart for him. While he was cooking the heart, a greasy splash hit Sigurd's thumb and he instantly put his thumb in his mouth. Suddenly, Sigurd could understand the speech of birds. The birds told him that Regin planned to kill Sigurd and that he, himself, should eat the heart and he would become very wise. Sigurd beheaded Reign for his betrayal and ate the heart. He became the wisest man in the land.

The story of Fafnir tells how the magick of the dragon is transferred to Sigurd and he can understand the speech of birds. Interesting observation: there is the theory that birds were created from the evolution of some dinosaurs; our prehistoric dragons. Could this be the reason why Sigurd is able to understand what the birds were saying? Eating the heart, of course, allows Sigurd the wisdom of the dragon. In our magical practice, we never harm dragons. We probably could not even if we wanted to. Instead, we can obtain this power of knowledge of the animals through sharing in the magick of the dragon.

Dragon Magick of Animals

In this technique, we will learn how to understand the language of animals. This magick can be of great help in our work with the animal kingdom. The more we understand animals, the more we can have a relationship with them. They can tell us many valuable things about themselves and the environment around them.

1. Use the trance dance or shaking and swaying seidr technique.
2. Send your consciousness down to the dragon below the earth.

3. Ask the dragon to help you connect, listen, and understand the voices of the animals and other wildlife.

4. While shaking and swaying, bring up the dragon consciousness into your body by taking deep breaths.

5. Bring the energy into your heart and your mind. Then send the dragon energy out of your heart in all directions. I like to visualize this as the dragon energy forming a sphere in my heart. As you exhale, allow the sphere to expand larger and larger until it encompasses the natural land around you. Allow this energy to connect with all the wildlife in your area.

6. Take a moment and listen to the animals, birds, and other wildlife. What are they saying? If you are having a hard time understanding them, send a little energy from your heart chakra to their heart chakra.

7. Introduce yourself and get to know them.

8. After a moment, thank the animals and disconnect from them.

9. When you are ready, thank the dragon and send the energy back underneath the earth.

10. Leave an offering for the dragon.

Eye of The Dragon

In magical tradition, the eye of the dragon has immense power. The dragon can see into space and time and has the power to see the fate strands on the Web of Wyrd. They can see what was, what is, and what will be. Some dragons are as old as the Universe itself and they know many things as well as things that shall come to pass. The dragon's eye can peer deep into the fabric of the universe and see the worlds of the stars and planets, the worlds of the dead, and the worlds of nature. The eye of the dragon has the power to alter the destinies of the human race at will. They can change the fates of humans for good or for ill. Witches and Spirit Walkers know of the powers of the dragon's eye. This magick is not for the beginner. Often times this magick requires the power of three witches to put the magick in motion. For those of us who have a relationship with the dragons, we are able to work this type of magick on our own. It is not so much about the power pouring through the witch or Spirit Walker, but rather how he or she is able to connect with the dragon energies.

To perform this magick is relatively easy. It is better to perform the Eye of the Dragon outside, but you can just as easily do this magick in your magical space as well. You will need to gather three sticks, each at least 18 inches in length, and arrange them in a triangle. The triangle is often used in magick to manifest energy. It also has the power to contain. Three sides equal three for Saturn which is the planetary energy of constriction and containing energy. You can use the Eye of the Dragon to gaze into the Web of Wyrd or two send out magick to do your Will.

Eye of the Dragon-To See

This is the magick to see into the past, present, or future. You will be conjuring the energies of the dragon to empower a vessel of water. You may use a black bowl or a small cauldron.

1. Place the scrying bowl or cauldron on the ground or table.
2. Place the three sticks around the vessel forming a triangle.
3. If you like, you may light dragon's blood incense to help in your magick.
4. If working in a group, everyone holds hands around the triangle. If working alone, place your hands on either side of the triangle making sure to touch the sticks.
5. Bring your consciousness down into the earth into the dragon's lair. Open your heart to the energies of the dragon.
6. You may use your own words or say, "**I call to you great Dragon! Come! Bring your energies into this sacred vessel so we may see the past, present, and future. Open**

your eyes and reveal to us the Web of Wyrd."

7. Sense that the dragon is coming up into the vessel. The opening of the container is the dragon's eye. Visualize the dragon opening his eye. Gaze into the dragon's eye. Ask your questions. Some answers may be revealed to you very clearly. Some may not. If this is the case, ask yourself: What do you see? What do you hear? What do you feel? What does your heart intuit?

8. When you are ready to send the dragon back to its lair say, **"Great Dragon. We thank you for your presence here. Close your eyes once more and go back to where you came. We shall call upon you again. Hail and farewell."**

9. Leave an offering for the dragon.

Eye of the Dragon- Spellcasting

This is the magick to conjure the dragon through sacred fire for spell casting. For this working, you will need three sticks and a vessel that can contain fire. You may use rubbing alcohol as your fuel. If outside, you can build a small bonfire on the ground.

1. Place your fire proof vessel on the table or on the ground, or if outside, build a small bonfire.

2. Place three sticks around the fire forming a triangle.

3. If using a vessel for fire, light it now. If working in a group, everyone should grab hands. If working along, place both hands on either side of the triangle.

4. Bring your consciousness down into the earth into the dragon's lair. Open your heart to the energies of dragon.

5. You may use your own words or say, **"I call you great dragon! Come! Come into this sacred vessel into the body of fire! Dance upon the flames! We ask that you manifest to us so we may work magick to place our Will upon the Web of Wyrd!"**

6. Spend a few moments visualizing the goal of your

magick. Think about it as clearly as you can. Speak the words to the dragon of that you wish to place into the Web of Wyrd. Tell the dragon the outcome you wish to achieve.

7. Visualize the dragon of fire leap up out of the vessel (or bonfire) and into the fabric of the Universe; into the Web of Wyrd to work your will.

8. When you are finished thank the dragon and leave an offering. You may speak from your heart or say the following, **"Great Dragon. We thank you for your presence here. Thank you for helping us work our Will on the Web of Wyrd. We shall call upon you again. Hail and farewell."**

9. Allow the fire to die down and go out.

Dragon Magick for Spellcasting

As we have learned, dragons are the magick and the power of the earth energy that flows from the deep earth up to the surface. When we connect to this powerful flow of energy through the dragon power, our magick and spells will be enhanced a great deal. In *Dragons: The Myths, Legends, and Lore,* Doug Niles gives us an example of how some dragons are willing to share their magick with us:

"In regions such as Bulgaria and Croatia, dragon myths took on a different tone from those of Russia and places farther north. In the south, dragons were considered to be very wise beings that were not necessarily enemies of mankind. They could use magic spells, and sometimes, if approached in the right way, they would share their knowledge."

In our spiritual practice, we know that to work with the power of the land we must have a special relationship with the earth and the beings that live upon her. As we work with the dragons, they will come to understand that we are healers and keepers of the earth mysteries. They will see that we seek to heal the earth and bring balance to the natural order of the Universe. Because of our dedication, many dragons will share their power and magick with us. I think it is important to really get to know your local dragons, great or small. As I have said, when we have a good relationship with the spirits, they are more willing to work with us and teach us of their magick. I will warn, though, that of all beings I have encountered, dragons are one of the most difficult to gain their trust. Once you do, there is much powerful magick that can be gained. Please remember that, with all spirits, we should not seek to have a relationship with them just for their magick. This is very unfair to them. Also, dragons will know your true intentions. There is a reason why in many stories you must approach mythological beings with a pure heart.

In order to gain the dragon power for spell casting, it is better to go to some place in nature where dragons can be found.

1. State your intention to seek out the dragon for magick.
2. Begin the shaking and swaying seidr technique.
3. Bring your consciousness down into the earth.
4. As you begin to shake and sway faster and faster, call upon the dragon energy to come up from the earth and into your body just as you did in the dragon invocation.
5. Bring the dragon energy into your heart and your consciousness. Take a moment to share energies with the dragon.
6. At this time, you may ask the dragon to teach you magick and enchantments. You can also ask them to add power to the ritual or spellcasting that you are performing. Once you have obtained the dragon energy and magick, you may continue to cast spells while shaking and swaying or you may stop the exercise.
7. When you are ready, thank the dragon for helping you in

magick. Make sure these thanks really come from a place of with heart-centered gratitude.
8. Feel the dragon energy recede from your body and back into the earth.
9. Leave an offering for the dragon.

Dragons can teach you many powerful acts of magick. By spending time with your dragon and continuing a healthy relationship with them, they will be more likely to share their magical talents with you. As I have said before, this may take quite some time. It is more important to connect with the dragons than it is to obtain their magical secrets.

Dragon Healing
Dragons have the ability to heal. They have great magick and with great magick there is healing. Healing can be physical, energetic, astral, or spiritual. Ideally, healing takes place on all of these levels. In holistic healing, you cannot heal one without healing the other. As we work with dragons and the energies of the land, we will learn more about our own spiritual and physical strengths and weaknesses. If we pay attention to the magick and energy around us we will see where we succeed and where we fail. Failing is just a part of magick and healing as our successes. The dragon current of energy will challenge you and this is where we find out who we are and which part of our lives we need to grow. For this healing magick, we will call upon the dragons of both fire and water. We will use the magick of draconic alchemy to blend the healing powers of water and fire to cleanse, heal, and restore our vitality. You will need a black bowl or cauldron and a fireproof container and rubbing alcohol.

1. Pour spring or filtered water into your black bowl or cauldron. Then place the alcohol in the fireproof container.

2. Place your hands over the bowl of water and say, **"I call upon the dragon of the watery deep. I ask that you come into and empower this sacred vessel with your magick."** Send your consciousness down into the depths of the earth that contains the waters below. See the water dragon come up from the watery depths of the earth into the bowl of water.

3. Place your hands over the fireproof container and say, **"I call upon the dragon of the fires of the earth. I ask that you come into and empower this sacred vessel with your magick."** Then light the alcohol. Send your consciousness down into the depths below the earth where lava and fire flow. See the dragon come up from the fires within the earth into the flame.

4. Then say, **"Dragon of water, Dragon of fire, I ask that your combine your energies and create the Healing Dragon Elixir. Blend your powers of water and fire for healing."**

5. Visualize the water dragon coming out of the bowl and the fire dragon coming out of the vessel. See them meet between the two containers and blend their magick to create a magical healing energy of fire and water combined. Know that is ancient alchemical process has powerful healing energies.

6. Then breath in this elixir into your heart chakra. You can send it to a specific area or send it to your entire body. You can also use this for someone else for distance healing. For distance healing, visualize the Alchemical Dragon Elixir to fly to the person you wish to send healing energy.

7. When you are finished thank the dragons for their magick. Then see the dragons disentangle. See the water dragon go back into the depths and the fire dragon return to its slumber in the earth below.

8. Thank the dragons for their magick and leave an offering.
9. Let the fire burn down and pour the water into a plant or pour outside.

The Dragon's Treasure

Many stories of dragons often speak of a great treasure that the mighty serpent is guarding or sometimes hoarding. They jealously guard gold and many other riches from any robber that may try to steal the treasure away from the dragon. More often than not, the would be robber is killed by the deadly dragon fire that awaits him. Through my experience of working with dragons, I have come to believe that the stories if dragons guarding treasure is a metaphor for two things. The first is that many dragons are creatures that live in the land and therefore guard the underground minerals and gems that naturally are formed within the earth. The second metaphor is that the actual treasure may not be physical gold but, rather, the earth's life force or ch'i that comes from deep within the land. The life force comes from the core of the earth as well as the mantle. This powerful force has the ability to create and sustain life and literally mover the surface of the earth. The life force can bring about all life on earth or it can destroy it. I believe this is what is meant when only a person "pure" or "innocent" of heart is able to take any of the treasure. Those of us who wish to help in the earth's healing are able to tap into the dragon's treasure of life force and use it to heal the wounds of the earth. Anyone who intends to misuse this great power for power over others will be met with the dragon's fire.

Conclusion

The Otherworld is full of magick. It has the power to heal and help us develop relationships with many Otherworld beings. As we have learned throughout this book, many of the legends and stories of the Otherworld are mysterious and strange. But once we have learned how to work with the Otherworld it is not as strange as we once thought. I have been working with the spirits of the land and the Otherworld for almost 30 years now. I have learned over time that what we humans think is odd, weird, or strange is quite normal to the Otherworld. The myths and stories are told to give us clues about the Elves, Faeries, Spirits, and Dragons. To most people, these stories are a warning to beware the mischievous Otherkin, but to the witch, these stories tell how to share powerful magick with the spirits of the land. When working with these wonderful and mysterious beings, we gain first-hand knowledge of how to connect and navigate the energies of the earth. With this knowledge we can heal ourselves as well as those who call upon us for help.

Wherever you live in the world, the land is sacred. If you live in a forest, coastal areas, deserts, mountains, or even in a large city, the land is sacred and each of the beings who reside there are magical. As witches, not only do we get our power from the moon and the stars, but we also receive power from the magick that flows from the land. As I end this book, I am reminded at the quote that opens Chapter One: Mother Earth.

"The Earth is your Grandmother and Mother, and She is sacred. Every step that is taken upon her should be a prayer."
Buffalo Calf Woman

Every single day we must remember that the earth is a living being. She is our Mother and she is a goddess. For many witches and pagans, she is the mother of all the gods. As I go through my daily life, I try to remember that as I walk down the sidewalk, I am being supported by the Earth Mother. As I drink water and eat my meals, they are from the Earth Mother. I try to remember to give thanks and to give her energy and healing back whenever I can. It is through the Earth Mother that I can connect with the spirits of the land. It is through her I can connect with the dragon energies that flow through her. We cannot have the Otherworld without the Earth Mother and we cannot have the Earth Mother without the Otherworld. Both are connected and both are holy. My final thought as I close out this book is this: Having a magical life is not just full moons and midnight rides with the Faeries. It is taking the magick and healing energies of the Otherworld beings and incorporating it into our daily lives so that every being upon the earth, that swims in the waters of the earth, and that flies in the skies of the earth can heal and be whole. In my Lakota teachings we say, "Mitakuye oyasin" which means "All my relations" or "We are all related". It is through this connectedness as spiritual relatives that we can heal and walk side by side with the beings of the Otherworld.

Bibliography

Allaun, Chris. *Deeper Into the Underworld: Death, Ancestors, and Magical Rites.* Mandrake of Oxford. 2017.

Allaun, Chris. *Upperworld: Shamanism and Magick of the Celestial Realm.* Mandrake of Oxford. 2019.

Barks, Coleman. *The Soul of Rumi: A New Collection of Ecstatic Poems.* Harper Collins. 2010.

Buhner, Stephen Harrod. *Sacred Plant Medicine: The Wisdom in Native American Herbalism.* Bear and Company. 2006.

Byock, Jesse L. *The Saga of the Volsungs: The Norse Epic of Sigurd the Dragon Slayer.* Penguin Classics.

Black Elk, Wallace H. and Lyon, William S. Ph.D. *Black Elk: The Sacred Ways of the Lakota.* HarperCollins Publishers. 1991.

Blain, Jenny. *Nine Worlds of Seid-Magic: Ecstacy and Neo-Shamanism in Northern European Paganism.* Routledge. 2002.

Blamires, Steve. *Magic of the Celtic Otherworld: Irish History, Lore, and Rituals.* Llewellyn Publications. 1995, 2007.

Brown, Joseph Epes. *The Sacred Pipe: Black Elk's Account of the Seven Rites of the Oglala Sioux.* University of Oklahoma Press. 1953, 1989.

Campbell, Joseph. *Romance of the Grail: The Magic and Mystery of Arthurian Myth.* New World Press. 2015.

Crow Dog, Leonard and Erdoes, Richard. *Crow Dog: Four Generations of Sioux Medicine Men.* Harper Perennial. 2012.

Daimler, Morgan. *Fairies: A Guide to the Celtic Fair Folk.* Moon Books. 2017.

Daimler, Morgan. *Fairycraft: Following the Path of Fairy Witchcraft.* Moon Books. 2015.

Daniel, Yvonne. *Dancing Wisdom: Embodied Knowledge in Haitian Vodou, Cuban Yoruba, and Bahain Candomble.* University of Illinois Press. 2005.

Devereux, Paul. *Spirit Roads: An Exploration of Otherworld Routes.*

Collins and Brown. 2003.

Evans-Wentz, W.Y. *The Fairy-Faith in Celtic Countries*. W.Y. Evans-Wentz. A Public Domain Book. 1911.

Farmer, Dr. Steven. *Spirit Animals as Guides, Teachers, and Healers*. Earth Magic, Inc. Publishing. 2016.

Filan, Kanaz. *The Haitian Vodou Workbook: Protocols for Riding with the Lwa*. Destiny Books. 2006.

Flowers, Stephen E and James A. Chisholm. Edited and Translated. *A Source-Book of Seid: The Corpus of Old Icelandic Texts Dealing with Seid and Related Words*. Lodestar. 2014.

Foxwood, Orion. *The Faery Teachings*. R.J. Stewart Books. 2007.

Friedlander, Shems. *The Whirling Dervishes*. State University of New York Press.

Fries, Jan. *Seidways: Shaking, Swaying and Serpent Mysteries*. Mandrake of Oxford. 1996.

Gary, Gemma. *Traditional Witchcraft: A Cornish Book of Ways*. Troy Books. 2008.

Gerrard, Katie. *Seidr The Gate is Open: Working with Trance Prophecy, The High Seat, and Norse Witchcraft*. Avalonia. 2011.

Green, Rosalyn. *The Magic of Shapeshifting*. Samuel Weiser, Inc. 2000.

Gundarsson, Kveldulf. *Elves, Wights, and Trolls: Studies Towards the Practice of Germanic Heathenry: Vol. I*. iUniverse. 2007.

Hall, Alaric. *Elves in Anglo-Saxon England*. The Boydell Press. 2007.

Hazen, Robert M. *The Story of Earth: The First 4.5 Billion Years, From Stardust to Living Planet*. Penguin Books. 2012.

Heaven, Ross and Charing, Howard G. *Plant Spirit Shamanism: Traditional Techniques for Healing the Soul*. Destiny Books. 2006.

Henkesh, Yasmin. *Trance Dancing with The Jinn: The Ancient Art of Contacting Spirits Through Ecstatic Dance*. Llewellyn Publications. 2016.

Ingersoll, Ernest. *Dragons and Dragon Lore*. Payson and Clarke Ltd. 1928.

John, Runic. *The Book of Seidr: The Native English and Northern European Shamanic Tradition.* Capall Bann. 2004.

Jones, Even John with Clifton, Chase S. *Sacred Mask Sacred Dance.* Llewellyn Publications. 1997.

Kaldera, Raven. *The Pathwalkers Guide to The Nine Worlds.* Asphodel Press. 2006.

Kelly, Michael. *Draconian Quadrilogy.* CreateSpace Independent Publishing Platform. 2014.

Kristin Andrews. *The Animal Mind: An Introduction to the Philosophy of Animal Cognition.* Routledge Publishing. 2015.

Lame Deer, Archie Fire and Erdoes, Richard. *Gift of Power: The Life and Teachings of a Lakota Medicine Man.* Bear and Company. 1992.

Laubin, Reginald and Laubin, Gladys. *Indian Dances of North American: Their Importance to Indian Life.* University of Oklahoma Press. 1977.

MacLeod, Sharon Paice. *Celtic Cosmology and the Otherworld: Mythic Origins, Sovereignty and Liminality.* 2018.

MacLeod, Sharon Paice. *Celtic Myth and Religion: A Study of Traditional Belief, with Newly Translated Prayers, Poems and Songs.* McFarland and Company, Inc. 2012.

Mails, Thomas E. *Fools Crow: Wisdom and Power.* Pointer Oak. 1991.

Mason, Asenath. *Draconian Ritual Book.* Megan Publications. 2016.

Matthews, Caitlin. *The Celtic Book of the Dead.* St. Martin's Press. 1992.

Matthews, Caitlin and John. *The Lost Book of the Grail: The Sevenfold Path of the Grail and the Restoration of the Faery Accord.* Inner Traditions. 2019.

Matthews, John. *The Sidhe: Wisdom from the Celtic Otherworld.* The Lorian Press. 2004, 2011.

Monroe, James S. and Wicander, Reed. *The Changing Earth: Exploring Geology and Evolution.* Cengage Learning. 2015, 2012.

Montgomery, Pat. *Plant Spirit Healing: A Guide to Working with*

Plant Consciousness. Bear and Company. 2008.

Mookerjee, Ajit. *Kundalini: The Arousal of The Inner Energy.* Destiny Books. 1982.

Neihardt, John G. *Black Elk Speaks: Being the Life Story of a Holy Man of the Oglala Sioux, The Premier Edition.* Excelsior Editions. 2008.

Niles, Doug. *Dragons: The Myths, Legends, and Lore.* Adams Media. 2013.

Paddon, Peter. *A Grimoire for Modern Cunning Folk.* Pendraig Publishing. 2011.

Sagan, Carl. *Dragons of Eden: Speculations on The Evolution of Human Intelligence.* Ballantine Books. 1977.

Sams, Jamie and Carson, David. *Medicine Cards.* St. Martin's Press. 1988, 1999.

Scott, Susan S. *Healing with Nature.* Helios Press. 2003, 2012.

Kinner, Stephen. *Feng Shui: The Living Earth Manual.* Tuttle Publishing. 2006,1982.

Stewart, R.J. *Earth Light: The Ancient Path to Transformation. Rediscovering the Wisdom of Celtic and Faery Lore.* Mercury Publishing. 1992, 1998.

Sullivan, Danny. *Ley Lines: The Greatest Landscape Mystery.* Green Magic. 2004.

Thorsson, Edred. *Witchdom of the True: A Study of the Vana-Troth and Roots of Seidr.* Runestar. 2018.

Ward, Peter and Kirschvink, Joe. *A New History of Life: The Radical New Discoveries About the Origins and Evolution of Life on Earth.* Bloomsbury Press. 2014.

Wilby, Emma. *Cunning Folk and Familiar Spirits: Shamanic Visionary Tradition in Early Modern British Witchcraft and Magic.* Sussex Academy Press. 2013.

Williams, Florence. *The Nature Fix: Why Nature Makes Us Happier, Healthier, and More Creative.* W. W. Norton and Company. 2017.

Websites and Links

(No Author listed. 2019. *Humpback Whales.* Journey North. (Online) Available at: https://journeynorth.org/tm/hwhale/SingingHumpback.html

Cronin, Aisling Maria. 2019. *These Five Stories of Amazing Times Wild Animals Saved People In Need Will Leave You Awe-Struck.* Onegreenplanet.org. (Online) Available at: https://www.onegreenplanet.org/animalsandnature/stories-of-amazing-times-wild-animals-saved-people-in-need/

Guarino, Ben. 2015. *Sea Lion Rescues Teenager Who Leaped Off Golden Gate Bridge.* Thedodo.com. (Online) Available at: https://www.thedodo.com/sea-lion-rescue-teenager-1023524523.html

Koch, Sarah-Neena. 2019. *Brain Evolution- The Triune Brain Theory.* MyBrainNotes.com. (Online) Available at: http://mybrainnotes.com/evolution-brain-maclean.html

Komninos, Andreas. 2017. *Our Three Brains- The Reptilian Brain.* Interaction Design Foundation (Online) Available at: https://www.interaction-design.org/literature/article/our-three-brains-the-reptilian-brain

Neil, Denise Ortuno. 2013. *Beware of the Tahquitz Witch.* Coachellavalleyweekly.com (Online) Available at: http://coachellavalleyweekly.com/beware-of-the-tahquitz-witch/

Peaco, Jim. 2019. *Grizzly Bear.* defenders.org. (Online) Available at: https://defenders.org/grizzly-bear/basic-facts

Prof. Geller. 2017. *Kitsune.* Mythology.net (Online) Available at: https://mythology.net/japanese/japanese-creatures/kitsune/

Sewall, Katie. 2015. *The Girl Who Gets Gifts from Birds.* BBC.Com/News. (Online) Available at: https://www.bbc.com/news/magazine-31604026

Shah, Amish. *Totem and the Practice of Totemism.* Projectyourself.com. (Online) Available at: https://projectyourself.com/blogs/news/totem-and-the-practice-of-totemism

University of Pittsburgh Schools of Health and Science. 2016. *New Insights into How the Mind Influences the Body.* sciencedaily.

com (Online) Available at: https://www.sciencedaily.com/ releases/2016/08/160815185555.htm

Articles

Maklin, Ruth. *Philosophy and Phenomenological Research Vol 39, No 2 pp. 155-181.* "Man's 'Animal Brains' and Animal Nature: Some Implications of a Psychophysiological Theory". International Phenomenological Society. 1978.

MOON
BOOKS

PAGANISM & SHAMANISM

What is Paganism? A religion, a spirituality, an alternative belief system, nature worship? You can find support for all these definitions (and many more) in dictionaries, encyclopaedias, and text books of religion, but subscribe to any one and the truth will evade you. Above all Paganism is a creative pursuit, an encounter with reality, an exploration of meaning and an expression of the soul. Druids, Heathens, Wiccans and others, all contribute their insights and literary riches to the Pagan tradition. Moon Books invites you to begin or to deepen your own encounter, right here, right now.

If you have enjoyed this book, why not tell other readers by posting a review on your preferred book site.

Recent bestsellers from Moon Books are:

Journey to the Dark Goddess
How to Return to Your Soul
Jane Meredith
Discover the powerful secrets of the Dark Goddess and
transform your depression, grief and pain into healing
and integration.
Paperback: 978-1-84694-677-6 ebook: 978-1-78099-223-5

Shamanic Reiki
Expanded Ways of Working with Universal Life Force Energy
Llyn Roberts, Robert Levy
Shamanism and Reiki are each powerful ways of healing; together,
their power multiplies. *Shamanic Reiki* introduces techniques to
help healers and Reiki practitioners tap ancient healing wisdom.
Paperback: 978-1-84694-037-8 ebook: 978-1-84694-650-9

Pagan Portals – The Awen Alone
Walking the Path of the Solitary Druid
Joanna van der Hoeven
An introductory guide for the solitary Druid, *The Awen Alone* will
accompany you as you explore, and seek out your own place
within the natural world.
Paperback: 978-1-78279-547-6 ebook: 978-1-78279-546-9

A Kitchen Witch's World of Magical Herbs & Plants
Rachel Patterson
A journey into the magical world of herbs and plants, filled with
magical uses, folklore, history and practical magic. By popular
writer, blogger and kitchen witch, Tansy Firedragon.
Paperback: 978-1-78279-621-3 ebook: 978-1-78279-620-6

Medicine for the Soul
The Complete Book of Shamanic Healing
Ross Heaven
All you will ever need to know about shamanic healing and how to
become your own shaman…
Paperback: 978-1-78099-419-2 ebook: 978-1-78099-420-8

Shaman Pathways – The Druid Shaman
Exploring the Celtic Otherworld
Danu Forest
A practical guide to Celtic shamanism with exercises and
techniques as well as traditional lore for exploring the Celtic
Otherworld.
Paperback: 978-1-78099-615-8 ebook: 978-1-78099-616-5

Traditional Witchcraft for the Woods and Forests
A Witch's Guide to the Woodland with Guided Meditations and
Pathworking
Mélusine Draco
A Witch's guide to walking alone in the woods, with guided
meditations and pathworking.
Paperback: 978-1-84694-803-9 ebook: 978-1-84694-804-6

Naming the Goddess
Trevor Greenfield
Naming the Goddess is written by over eighty adherents and
scholars of Goddess and Goddess Spirituality.
Paperback: 978-1-78279-476-9 ebook: 978-1-78279-475-2

Shapeshifting into Higher Consciousness
Heal and Transform Yourself and Our World with Ancient
Shamanic and Modern Methods
Llyn Roberts
Ancient and modern methods that you can use every day to
transform yourself and make a positive difference in the world.
Paperback: 978-1-84694-843-5 ebook: 978-1-84694-844-2

Readers of ebooks can buy or view any of these bestsellers by
clicking on the live link in the title. Most titles are published in
paperback and as an ebook. Paperbacks are available in traditional
bookshops. Both print and ebook formats are available online.

Find more titles and sign up to our readers' newsletter at
http://www.johnhuntpublishing.com/paganism
Follow us on Facebook at https://www.facebook.com/MoonBooks
and Twitter at https://twitter.com/MoonBooksJHP